D1508849

Early Widow

A Journal of the First Year

Mary Jane Worden

INTERVARSITY PRESS
DOWNERS GROVE, ILLINOIS 60515

InterVarsity Press is the book-publishing division of InterVarsity Christian Fellowship, a student movement active on campus at hundreds of universities, colleges and schools of nursing. For information about local and regional activities, write Public Relations Dept., InterVarsity Christian Fellowship, 6400 Schroeder Rd., P.O. Box 7895, Madison, WI 53707-7895.

Distributed in Canada through InterVarsity Press, 860 Denison St., Unit 3, Markham, Ontario L3R 4H1, Canada.

ISBN 0-8308-1219-9

Printed in the United States of America

Library of Congress Cataloging-in-Publication Data
Worden, Mary Jane, 1946-
    Early widow: a journal of the first year/Mary Jane Worden;
  foreword by Gladys M. Hunt.
      p. cm.
    ISBN 0-8308-1219-9
      1. Worden, Mary Jane, 1946-   --Diaries.   2. Widows--United
  States--Diaries.   3. Bereavement.   I. Title.
  HQ1058.5.U5W67   1989
306.8'8--dc19   89-1721
                                                                       CIP

16   15   14   13   12   11   10   9   8   7   6   5   4   3   2
99   98   97   96   95   94   93   92   91   90   89

For John M. Worden,
Jim's father

Foreword

The world has widened for Mary Jane Worden (née Peterson) as the years have passed. She began life as the second of six children in a small logging and farming town (population about 250) in the north woods of Michigan. Her father's timber business made him a major employer, and commitment to the church made them one of the town's first families. Her high-school class had twenty-seven graduates; the school wasn't large enough to produce a football team for the area league.

But small beginnings offer their own kind of security and dreams. One of these dreams began coming true when Mary Jane went on a vacation with family friends and came to InterVarsity's Cedar Campus. The tall, dark, handsome man of her adolescent fantasies was not only on the site but, *mirabile dictu,* he seemed interested in her. He was the ultimate in world-wideners for this high-school senior, and her life became intricately woven into his. You cannot relate to Mary Jane's sense of loss without knowing something of Jim, for it is in his company that she became the person she is today.

I read somewhere that "grieving is accentuated by the endearing qualities of the deceased." It was right after Jim Worden had been killed in a head-on collision by a drunk-drugged driver on a Texas highway in April 1983. My mind flooded with images and feelings of warmth and love. *It's true,* I thought, *that's why the loss of Jim has torn apart our hearts and left us so desolate.*

I know the tendency to give to the dead qualities they never possessed in life and to sentimentalize reality. Sudden loss can make you forget the pain, the hurt, the failures of the past, and maybe that is a healing thing for some people. But reality was different with Jim Worden. He seemed born with an extra supply of loveable traits—a charmer, if you will, but in the most honest and natural sense of that word. Somehow he was just comfortable being who he was—a man of substance and easy manner.

It is no simple thing to describe that kind of person. The words available don't do the job. Eyes that softened when he talked to you; a delighted look that warmed his smile; a disarming way that made you feel you were special; a right mixture of affability and comeliness. He was tall, attractive, masculine; but those are only facts, not why we loved him.

My husband and I first met Jim when he was a freshman at the University of Wisconsin in Madison. He had come to Michigan to attend a training session at InterVarsity Christian Fellowship's Cedar Campus, a camp for university students. I'd probably have to look at a list to remember anyone else who was at that camp with the clarity with which I remember Jim—with his youthful honesty, his intention to be a disciple of Jesus Christ back on campus, his participation in discussions, and his fun-loving ways. Emotionally my husband and I adopted him as our own, and following his college career and spiritual growth was easy because he kept coming back to see us. My husband liked the discernment and spiritual maturity he saw in him, and when Jim graduated he asked him to become a campus staff member for InterVarsity at Michigan State University.

InterVarsity Christian Fellowship is an interdenominational student ministry on university and college campuses in the United States. When Jim came to work for InterVarsity he never dreamed student work would be his career. He began as a campus staff member, later becoming the Michigan area director. When he moved to Texas in 1975 he became the Southwest regional director. In that role he also led the evangelism project at Breckenridge, Colorado, that Mary Jane mentions in her journal, and later he became the director of Bear Trap Ranch, also in Colorado. Jim's Christian commitment, his insistence on integrity and truth, and his solid biblical convictions were the makings of a man of God. In his fifteen years on staff, he influenced the lives of hundreds of students.

Jim Worden met Mary Jane Peterson during his freshman

year on his first visit to Cedar Campus. The attraction was mutual, and they developed a relationship with each other in a somewhat casual way over the next four years. Mary Jane's parents had tracts of land with streams for fishing and woods for hunting—all things Jim enjoyed—but Mary Jane was the prime drawing card. He became part of the Peterson family before he ever married into it. It was such a comfortable arrangement that he might have delayed marriage for some time if Mary Jane hadn't felt it was time to decide if he was committed to her family or to her. He was going to be a staff member at the university she was attending; why not get married now? Jim, in his laid-back fashion, thought it was a good idea and in the flurry of his graduation left getting the license and the dime-store wedding rings to Mary Jane, which would have been a disastrous beginning to a marriage if Jim hadn't been so guileless about the whole thing. Many years later, when Mary Jane had children but still no proper wedding ring, we had a little talk together—Jim and I—and I gave him a woman's point of view on such unromantic happenings. The next time I saw them, he proudly showed me a gold ring he had fashioned for her, with his thumb prints embedded in the gold. It's not fair to say he wasn't a romantic; he just expressed it in surprising ways and with his inimitable timing.

Timing was part of who Jim Worden was, and sometimes it wasn't one of his strong points. He was a people person, no doubt of that. He lost all sense of time when engaged in conversations, which often exasperated his family as well as his secretary. He would race along in his car at a good and purposeful clip until he started to tell a story. Then, quite unaware, he might poke along at thirty-five miles per hour while elaborating the fine points of his tale. A history aficionado, he sketched out the entire battleground of Little Big Horn with a Magic Marker on the car windows while riding with staff members from Bear Trap Ranch to Denver one day. When they stopped at a gas station, the attendant inquired what that was all over his windows. Jim shrugged, "Oh, just the Battle of Little Big Horn." No one in the car will ever forget that drive. I can't imagine anyone not liking his company.

Jim owned a very-used Land Rover, a used Mad River Canoe and a Parker 12-gauge shotgun. He gave Mary Jane a Browning .22 rifle for her birthday one year, which didn't excite her particularly. While his outdoor enthusiasm attracted her, she learned quickly that that was not who she was. Jim led wilderness canoe trips out of Cedar Campus for several years. An adventurer at heart, he would spend hours perusing maps, charting trails in the middle of nowhere. On one occasion, he and our son Mark sat up until the wee hours one morning only to have Mary Jane wake up and announce that it was time to go to the hospital for their second child to be born.

Jim had multiple talents. He was an artist, inheriting his father's gift, and then passing his creativity on to his children. He never quite found time to do all the things he was interested in before his life was cut short at age thirty-seven. His colorful word choices made for interesting conversation; he was well-informed about many subjects, a good speaker and discussion leader. His sense of humor, his clever quips, his world view were all part of the appeal of this man. Playing his banjo with a limited repertoire, he'd sing, "Lay some happiness on me." He attracted people to him like bees to honey.

The marriage of Jim and Mary Jane was a good one—two people made for each other. From the first she adapted to his demanding schedule, entertaining staff and students, making a charming home on a minimal salary, trotting off to camp with him and making new friends. They had to work on belonging to each other and giving each other space the way everyone else does. It wasn't always easy or perfect; it was a real marriage between two real people.

When Jeff was born we danced around the room for joy, and Jim beamed over his beautiful son. Jessie came next and fussed about life until she could walk and talk, a verbal child who since learning to read has been consuming books as if she were a vacuum cleaner. Jim was charmed with her early creativity. Ethan was Texas-born, laid-back from birth, a homespun philosopher. Beautiful kids, a good family with good parents.

The strength of Jim's personality made it almost inevitable that Mary Jane would defer to him and to his wishes. She was only twenty when she married him, and not as certain about who she was and what she could do as Jim was. Jim's personality made this an easy relationship. Mary Jane majored in hospitality; she easily included others in their family life; she was full of her own good works. But in many ways, though I never thought of this at the time, the star of the show was Jim. He just happened to have a wonderful supporting cast.

When news of Jim's death reached the host of people who

loved him, the outpouring of grief and sympathy for Mary Jane was overwhelming. He was not only far too special to die so soon, but what would Mary Jane do without him? Probably few widows have had so much sympathy. For none of us knew what we would do without him, but Mary Jane and the children. . . .

In the goodness of God, Mary Jane's sister Lin had come to Texas several months earlier to live with the Wordens, and she now took on the task of helping Mary Jane bear her grief. Lin may seem to be a background figure in the story, but much of what Mary Jane writes would be vastly different without her. She took up the family reins: she fed the children, comforted everyone, kept the household moving. Probably even Mary Jane in her grief did not realize all that Lin was doing. Few widows have the luxury of such a special gift. She gave Mary Jane the space and time to grieve. Numerous kind people met numerous needs. I remember Lin saying, "Sometimes Christ comes to you in the form of other people."

Mary Jane may have wondered whose friend all of these people were, but she found out in a hurry. They were *her* friends; and she found out things about herself, about God's care and love, about her own abilities, about the quality of her "believing" that she may never have known before. She did not suddenly become a woman of spiritual strength; she *had been becoming* all through these years of growing and caring and studying the Bible. Truth larger than her small self flooded her life, and we were all instructed by it.

She came back to Michigan to be with us at Cedar Campus that first summer after Jim's death, and then the next summer and the next. It was obvious what God was doing in her life in making her whole and giving her a ministry. She gave several workshops on facing grief, and we saw how helped others were by her honest words. She had not put grief on the back burner; she had made work of it and came out refined.

And so it was that I took her out to lunch one day and suggested that she take her journal and make a book from it. The idea began to grow and we went away together for a week to a friend's condominium on the shore of Lake Michigan and began the project. We cried together, and prayed, and she started writing. She has a way with words that lets you into her life, and that is what makes this book so fresh and real.

I must confess that it is hard for me to be objective because this family has such a large place in my heart. It didn't seem to me a good plan to take away a fine father from his three children and leave a vulnerable wife bereft. But I was not asked. I could only trust with everyone else. What I have seen come out of what the world calls a human tragedy is more than enough to assure me of the mercy and grace of God. God is in the business of fitting all of us for eternity, and I commend to you the story of his grace in one remarkable woman's life.

Gladys M. Hunt

Preface

I like boxes with neatly tied ribbons, stories with happy endings and dilemmas which come to quick and clean resolu-
tions.

This journal isn't like that because it depicts real people
living in a real world. It is a chronicle of the first year in my
life as a young widow. In the midst of struggling to pick up
the pieces of my shattered family, I learned to do the work
of grieving. Taken from my journals, with occasional altera-
tions of name or circumstance, it is a candid accounting of
the trials and terrors of our journey into the unfamiliar realm
of the bereaved. But it also depicts the faithfulness of God as
we made our way through that year of grief.

I have written not just for the bereaved. You may be struggling to help someone you love through this difficult process

of grieving; you will find here a wealth of suggestions and ideas as you read of the many ways our friends reached out to us in love.

But perhaps more than all else, I wish to write to people in everyday relationships, encouraging you in the hard work of intimacy, urging you to make the most of the days given and helping you to see that all of life is a gift.

We all suffer losses of various kinds in our lives: broken relationships, relocations which leave behind friends and familiar places, disappointments, unmet expectations and unfulfilled dreams. But we have an amazing facility for pain-avoidance, and the result may be that we carry an accumulating burden of emotional baggage that prevents us from living life fully and well.

During the nearly sixteen years of my marriage I had read a lot of books about death and bereavement, partly to be prepared to comfort others, partly perhaps to ward off such pain in my own life. As I faced the tragedy of Jim's unexpected death, I knew, from somewhere deep inside me, that there was grief-work to be done. I was determined, in those early days, to devote myself to that process, even though I had few clues as to what that really meant. In retrospect I see how invaluable that deliberate approach has been to us, how much healing God has brought as we've actively worked at grieving.

I began the journal within a day or two of Jim's death, knowing I would want a record of the events of those first weeks. But I find that my journal-keeping is largely a record of personal reflections and feelings—events are simply hooks on which to hang the real stuff of life. With a few additions and modifications for clarity, the text is taken almost directly from the journals. My eagerness to share this personal account of that year in our family's life is rooted in the deep hope that our experience might somehow model to others that work of grief—not the ideal method but rather the fact of its necessity. I'm increasingly convinced that grieving is work which must be done if we are not to be enslaved by the past.

There is no formula for adequate grief-work; the process will be different for everyone. The primary ingredient, I think, is to face the reality of our pain, to determine to put our energies into dealing with the sadness rather than into trying to avoid it. Our Western culture teaches us to minimize discomfort at all costs, to distract ourselves, to mask the pain. I urge you instead to face it, to name it, to allow yourself to feel the sadness and acknowledge your loss. Spend time thinking about it, talking about it. Immerse yourself in it for a time. But don't run away from it. You may find some of your own unresolved grief coming to the surface if you allow yourself to be drawn into our story as you read. If you can, give yourself permission to feel that pain and cry those tears. Tears are cleansing, and on the other side of deep pain we can find healing for our brokenness, growth toward wholeness, even great joy.

Mary Jane and Jim Worden with their three children (left to right), Jessica, Jeff and Ethan (March 1983).

$$I$$

April 29, 1983   Friday   *Austin, Texas*

I pick up the telephone, groggy with sleep. *Who would be calling at one in the morning?* "This is the emergency room nurse at Caldwell County Hospital. Your husband has been fatally injured in a car accident." I am instantly alert and awake. *What does fatally injured mean? He's dying? already dead?* I feel the words as a physical blow, as though someone has kicked me in the stomach. With unexpected composure I ask to speak to the doctor. *It is true. Jim is dead.* Questions asked, information exchanged.

Was Jim driving the car? No, the doctor is reasonably certain that he hadn't been. Then Pete must have been driving. Critically injured, Pete needs an orthopedic surgeon's care immediately. His parents, who live in Montana, will be notified.

Arrangements are made to have him transferred to an Austin hospital.

The doctor's final question undoes me: "And what shall we do with your husband's body?"

I hang up the telephone, engulfed by a kaleidoscope of emotions. *My life with Jim is over. Nineteen years of loving and being loved. Finished.* Alongside that searing pain of loss comes a surprising sense of completion, of closure. Our life together has come to a shattering, abrupt end, yet somehow it feels settled, finished. We have done and said the important things. There isn't unfinished business between us.

My mouth is so dry. Cottonmouth. It reminds me of an experience last summer, my first attempt at rock-climbing. As my mind does a flashback to that scene in Colorado, I remember my terror as I stood at the bottom of what appeared to be straight-up rock wall. And I remember the security of being "on belay," roped safely to an experienced mountaineer-coach at the top. *I may be frightened, but I know I'm safe.*

My sister Lin comes into my room. Having listened on the other phone, she has the Caldwell Hospital's telephone number, seventy-five miles away. How could I have coped with this crisis alone? How providential that she "just happens" to be living with us this year. Hugging and sobbing, words are unnecessary, inadequate.

She calls Tim, a neighbor and friend. As a doctor he is accustomed to being awakened by emergency calls. But three times he asks her to repeat the message; his mind refuses to accept the fact of his friend's death. Within a few minutes he and his wife, Kathy, arrive to spend the next hours with us. Their willingness to suffer alongside us somehow enables me to bear the intolerable.

Others have to be informed of Jim's death. Several calls are made immediately: to my parents in Michigan, to Jim's family in Wisconsin. Others can be called in the morning. Making those lists occupies some of the hours before dawn, but eventually I have to face it: *How can I tell the children that their daddy is never coming home again?* All three are heavy sleepers; I opt to wait until morning to tell them. My own deep grief is upstaged by the anticipated agony of bearing this news to them.

Encircled on our bed, pajama-clad, sleep and puzzlement in their eyes, they wait for me to speak. I reach out to my three chicks, wanting to draw them into the shelter of my wings. A deep breath, tears in my voice: "I have something very important to tell you. But first I want you to remember that God loves us very much, and he doesn't allow bad things to happen without being there to hold us up. A very bad thing has happened. . . ." Looks of shock and surprise, questions, tears.

Twelve-year-old Jeff takes the sharp-edged pain inside of himself, the enormity of his loss known only to him. But I can see it brimming in his eyes. Jessica has learned in her ten years (from her mother?) to try to gain mastery over life's events by wrapping words around them. But there aren't enough words, or they aren't big enough, to protect us from this monstrous fact. Protests and denials are powerless to alter or negate this painful event. At five, Ethan is unable to grasp the reality and finality of such a pronouncement. A nervous giggle escapes his lips. Remembering my similar response to my grandfather's death many years before, I reach out to touch him, not wanting him to be embarrassed by a sense of inappropriateness. Protected somehow by his youth, he will find the pain coming more slowly to him.

We step, wounded, into the day.

The day has only just begun, but there is a bustle in the house. Doorbells, phone calls, food, flowers, telegrams—so many expressions of caring. Bill, the lawyer, comes from across the street to assure me that he will handle all of our legal and financial details; his voice is sad and quiet and strong. He is followed by his wife, Carolyn, her cleaning lady in tow; together the two women tackle my dirty bathrooms.

Jim's assistant, Ann, arrives and is greeted on the porch by Jessie, her arms open wide and tears streaming: "Ann, my daddy is dead." Ann can no longer hope to disbelieve the news she had heard by telephone not long before. Coming inside, she takes up her usual post at her desk in Jim's office, across from his now-vacant chair. For most of the day she is on one or both telephones, carefully recording all messages. Along with the many words of condolence come friends' thoughtful offers of help: "I have room in my home for two guests." "Would Ethan like to come play with Kyle?" "Can I pick someone up at the airport?" Ann distinguishes herself as Master Listmaker.

Another listmaker, Lin, is beside me every moment that I am not resting. I find that my brain is on overload: any thought not immediately spoken aloud for Lin to write down is lost forever. *Jessie needs shoes for the funeral. The library books are overdue.* A collage of details that says life must go on.

Dr. Tim, bringing regular hospital reports on Pete's condition, is a rock of comfort and information. Kathy and Carolyn are gearing up my kitchen in anticipation of several dozen guests for the weekend.

Ethan wants to go to his preschool but inexplicably balks at riding with the neighbor. I go along and walk with him to his classroom to talk to his teacher. "I want you to know this so you will believe it if he tells you: Ethan's daddy was killed in a head-on collision with a drunk driver last night." It is the first time (other than with the children) I have spoken those words face to face; they hang suspended in the air like giant icicles. Ethan's teacher reaches through to hug me, shattering the brittle barrier, and says with quiet tears and remembering in her voice, "My dad died when I was about Ethan's age."

At some point in the morning I walk into the boys' room to check on Jeff. He looks up from his pillow. "Mommy, what about the other person?"

"There weren't any others in the car, only Daddy and Pete."

"No, I mean in the other car—the driver. Is he okay?" I am deeply moved by his extension of concern, and I am shamed. It hadn't even occurred to me to ask.

At 2:30 we go to the funeral home—doctor, lawyer, widow, pastor. Both Tim and Bill know the owner personally and have called to pave my way. "This family has built a deliberately simple lifestyle and that is their strong preference now: simplicity." Signing papers; discussing costs; recalling details of Jim's birth, life and death for his obituary. *What else do I want included? How do I know—I've never read the obituaries.*

Based primarily on pragmatic reasons, and having received the consent of his parents, I have chosen to have Jim's body cremated. I remember our brief and inconclusive discussions about this—now the decision must be mine alone. I inquire about seeing his body. They strongly urge me not to "because of the nature of his injuries. . . ." *Well, if I don't see him, none of the family can. That eliminates one dilemma.*

To assure myself that I won't at some later, irrational moment question whether it was really Jim, I ask Tim to look at his body. My inquiry about Jim's wedding band brings the response, "We may have to saw the ring to enable us to remove it from his hand." I turn again to Tim. "You're a surgeon. Do what you must, but I'd like to have his ring." Why would they saw through the ring if the body is to be burned tomorrow? I'm trying to remind myself in every way that this is only a body, a shell, no longer useful. Jim has returned to his Creator. In a few minutes Tim is back, fresh sadness in his eyes, a misshapen but whole ring in his hand.

Starting down the steps in the bright sunlight, I falter a bit and reach for the porch pillar. Strong arms encircle me. Such tenderness and deference prompt more tears.

Hours later family and friends begin to arrive from the airport. The world is a troubled place. My parents come to my room, distraught to be the bearers of more pain: my cousin died this afternoon. *At thirty-seven, Jim was two years younger than Roy; as they begin their Real Life, he's one day older.* Although I knew that Roy was seriously ill, I am still stunned. My heart aches for Priscilla and her three young children. *I thought broken was broken. How can a heart sustain more pain? Priscilla, long one of my favorite people, is far away. Two widows and six children out on the roiling sea; if only we could reach each other to lash our flimsy crafts together . . .*

A friend calls across many miles to assure me that, from God's perspective, this is Plan A for us, not Plan B. And Ann points out David's words in Psalm 46:

God is our refuge and strength,
an ever-present help in trouble.
Therefore we will not fear, though the earth give way
and the mountains fall into the heart of the sea,
though its waters roar and foam
and the mountains quake with their surging.

Timely words, and comforting. I feel my world crumbling around me, and yet I know that I am loved by the God who is in control of the universe.

Food is urged on me; I have no appetite. I force myself to eat a few bites—nourishing perhaps, but without taste. I have lain down to rest several times today, but sleep has not come. Instead, my mind is flooded with memories, my eyes with tears. I am terribly weary. Tim insists that I take a sleeping pill. I resist; the good doctor wins.

It was morning, and it was evening, the first day. The first day, and new beginnings: an empty bed and a world of pain.

April 30   Saturday

I waken early; awareness is immediate. A sense of desolation and loss sweeps over me as I turn to the emptiness beside me. Jim is gone. In my mind I re-create his body: tall, strong, healthy; his long-lashed eyes, firm jaw; his beautiful dark, thick hair—I long to put my fingers in his hair again. I weep because I had often imagined what lovely, full white hair he would have in a few years, like his Grandfather Stiles.

Later in the morning it occurs to me that I would like to have some sort of committal service with the children, beside Jim's body at the funeral home. Inquiry reveals that cremation has already begun. That gives me some bad moments. . . . When I think of his body—damaged, distorted, broken, burned—I ache in a special way with the awareness of what deep pleasure we enjoyed with one another's body.

Several of us meet with the minister to plan the funeral service. A mild flash of anger: *You did it to me! You went off and left me to do this by myself! How many times had I asked you to sit down with me to plan our funerals?* We decide to use as a memorial folder the Christmas card which Jim had designed and produced. *How long had it lain, almost finished, in your desk drawer?* Originally intended as an Easter card, the addition of a sprig of holly to the crown of thorns adapted it nicely to the Christmas season. *Just a few months ago we had spent those hours beside the fire, writing notes, signing cards, addressing envelopes; even the children had helped by coloring in the holly berries with marking pens.* A multi-use card, flexible, adaptable, it reflects Jim's character and gifts in a variety of ways. Inside the card we add the words of 1 Thessalonians 4:13, 18: "We want you not to remain in ignorance, brothers, about those who sleep in death; you should not grieve like the rest of men, who have no hope. We believe that Jesus died and rose again; and so it will be for those who died as Christians; God will bring them to life with Jesus. . . . Thus we shall always be with the Lord. Console one another, then, with these words" (NEB).

In the afternoon Kathy, Tim's wife, arrives with several of her dresses for me to try on, suggesting I borrow one for the funeral. She says, "I wore one of my favorite dresses to my mother's funeral, and I haven't been able to wear it since." I am touched by her thoughtfulness, but I feel that somehow I will be less "present" if I wear someone else's clothes. It reminds me of praying with Jim before our wedding that we would feel very present, fully aware and able to deeply enjoy those special moments of beginning our marriage. The beginning, and now the end of our life together. Again that prayer, an echo. But there's a hollowness to it. Jim has gone. The joy has gone.

Ethan's bath time is supervised tonight by Paul, a friend who builds him a boat from an empty tissue box. Life still holds its small pleasures. He comes, sweet-smelling and scrubbed, into the office where I am sitting at Jim's desk. He climbs into my lap and says, "Mommy, now there are only four people in our family." (Numbers hold great fascination to one who is learning to count, and Ethan delights in assigning quantitative value to his world.)

"Yes, that's true, but we do have lots and lots of friends."

"I know, and maybe someday . . ." (his voice drops to a whisper as he realizes he's being overheard) "maybe someday one of Daddy's friends will want to be my daddy." *I'm sure Paul's wife won't think much of that idea.*

"Well, perhaps so—but we don't have to decide tonight."

"You're right, Mom. We can decide tomorrow."

Smiles through my tears. There must be hope if one can smile. But so far the tears are winning.

Morning and evening, the second day.

May 1   Sunday

Midmorning I find myself out in the garden, watering tomato plants. My gardens have never been spectacular successes, and this one needs more than a good watering. Somehow there is comfort, a soothing of my soul, in this place today. I have an almost desperate sense of wanting to touch something real, solid, connected to the earth. Salt tears mingle with fresh water from the garden hose.

Friends are still arriving, some from far places. I see them in clusters, in the back yard, throughout the house. This house was made for people, lots of them, and it gives me pleasure to see it full of life at this time of death. *How I wish you could be here to enjoy this gathering of your favorite people, Jim.*

Jim's parents arrive from the airport and I greet them on

the front lawn. We share our mutual loss. Tears say more than words. It is terribly difficult for them. There's something out of the natural order of things when a child precedes his parents in death.

Word comes from the hospital that Pete's crisis has passed despite a life-threatening embolism. . . . There were many "effectual, fervent prayers." *God, help us all.*

The children are asking some hard questions. "If Daddy's in heaven where there's no sadness or crying, how can he be happy if he sees how sad we are?" *Where is my answer book? Who am I to try to explain, even sometimes to understand for myself, the ways of God?*

In a few short days (and probably some long nights), our friend Charles, a violin maker, has transformed once-ordinary pieces of wood into a work of art. My request that he make a box to hold the container of ashes was prompted by an article I had recently read. A community of believers prepared together for a member's impending death from cancer by building a pine coffin and piecing a quilt in which to wrap his body. I like the idea of friends actively participating in this "rite of passage."

And this is no ordinary box. It is a masterpiece of cherry and birds-eye maple, lovingly and painstakingly crafted by Charles and our mutual friend Charlie. It has the sheen of a fine violin. My brother has thoughtfully brought a small goose which he carved; it "flies" nicely atop The Box, one wing dipped in salute. *How you would have delighted in the beauty of this piece, Jim; it would meet, and exceed, even your perfectionist's standards.*

For the funeral I choose to wear my new white blouse—not exactly widow's black mourning garb. It was one of my rare "solo" purchases, and I was delighted by Jim's obvious approval. *What was it you said after I wore it to that party a few weeks ago? "I enjoyed being with you. You were the loveliest lady there." "Really?" "Easily."* Not exactly a party, but I do wish for this funeral to be not simply an acknowledgment of his death, but also—somehow—a celebration of Jim's life.

The church is crowded with friends, family and people touched by Jim's life. We are among the last to enter the sanctuary. I am disappointed to have missed most of the Pachelbel Canon, one of Jim's favorites. *The glorious music was one of the reasons we were drawn to this church, wasn't it?*

Just before the service begins, the children and I lay a bright red amaryllis on top of The Box. We had picked it from our garden—four lovely blossoms on a strong green stem. *Symbolic somehow of four relative innocents facing the harsh reality of a fallen world?*

The children sit quietly. Our profusion of tears are erratic, unrelated, occasional. I'm grateful that someone has thoughtfully brought pencils and paper. My budding artists can sit through even a lengthy service like this one if they are allowed to draw.

I am caught by the unexpected, drowning in my tears. Jessica has asked them to play "Edelweiss," remembering it as one of Daddy's favorites. I remember that it had been a part of our wedding. I struggle to sing "God Is Our Refuge"; it feels like I'm blowing bubbles in my throat. Based on Psalm 46, this was a song Jim had, with unknowing foresight, taught the family.

The liturgy brings comfort. The Scriptures. The sermon and prayers. The Eucharist. All remind me that One is in charge who can be trusted. He loves us and intends good for us.

We move into the Parish Hall after the service. A table, lovely in its simplicity of white cloth and white flowers, graces the center of the room. I move from hug to hug, words of sadness and hope, shared tears. Someone touches my shoulder and says, "I think Jeff needs you." I turn to see my son with head in hands, sobbing, his two best friends on either side. A vigil of love. My heart breaks to see his grief, and aches with pride that he is man enough to weep in front of his friends.

Tears are cleansing. And exhausting. Tonight I will sleep.

II

May 2   Monday

T he early mornings are proving to be the weepiest for me. I've always awakened early, and my mind becomes quickly active. It's a good time to cry—not angry, frustrated tears (yet) but sometimes quiet tears, sometimes wrenching sobs, usually prompted by a special memory or a jolting reminder of his death. Like remembering our last evening out together. Just last week: dessert at a neighborhood cafe, a leisurely walk home, conversation and cuddling in the hammock. . . .

This morning I went with Bill to the bank to open the safe-deposit box. We were graciously met by an officer of the bank; again Bill has called to prepare the way. Later, a council of family advisers met in Jim's office to discuss legal matters. Bill entered, papers in hand, to say, "I have examined the will and find everything as it ought to be." I felt a rush of relief and gratitude, surprised at the sweetness of those words. *If my troubles were compounded by tangled legal affairs, how could I bear it?*

Bill gave us a preliminary financial statement. "This is what we know today to be the anticipated insurance, pension and Social Security benefits. It's not the final word." *Numbers on a piece of paper. They won't compute for me. The Final Word: will it be poverty? I don't want rich; just tell me we won't be desperate.*

One of the Scriptures read last night echoes in my mind: "They will be called oaks of righteousness, a planting of the LORD for the display of his splendor" (Is 61:3). *Can I pray that this will be a strengthening experience for us? To all appearances a tragedy, a family destroyed. But in God's economy an opportunity to build into four lives marks of his character. Lord, grow these four saplings into Oaks of Righteousness for your glory.*

Someone came to me to say, "Remember, you have friends all around the world who are praying for you and your children." That struck a deep chord for me; it continues to resonate as I prepare for bed. Our friends in Japan are still awake, and before they sleep those in Spain will be rising. The words from a familiar hymn come to mind:

"We thank Thee that Thy church unsleeping, While earth rolls onward into light, Throughout all the world her watch is keeping, And rests not now by day or night. . . . The day thou gavest, Lord, is ended."

May 3   Tuesday

A flight to Madison, a second funeral service. This time among the InterVarsity coworkers. From Texas to Wisconsin, from wife to widow—I am worlds away from where I was just five days ago.

Tim asked about our travel plans. "We leave this morning, the funeral will be tonight and I will try to return tomorrow." "I don't want to see you back here before Friday." "But my children need me!" "Your children need you to come back rested. And your parents will take fine care of them while you're gone." Lin and I will return on Friday.

Someone found waterproof mascara in the airport shop at my request. I feel not-quite-dressed without at least a little eye makeup; my current stuff has no staying power. On those occasions when I had considered the possibility of this ever happening to me (*Does every woman do that when her husband is late?*) I had imagined a new widow to be oblivious to details of hair, makeup, clothing. I'm surprised to find myself feeling even a little concerned about my appearance.

My sense of vulnerability is high. As I stepped onto the plane I had an irrational urge to knock on the door of the cockpit: "You have no idea how important it is that you get me there safely. I simply *must* get back to my three children." Last night both Jeff and Jessie expressed their fears about my leaving. Another hard question: "Why should we ask God to keep you safe? We always prayed that for Daddy." Again my understanding is too limited for these hard things.

Jeff asked me to come into his room before he went to sleep last night. He really didn't want me to go away—because I might not return, and because he didn't think he could talk and cry with anyone else. So we talked and cried. I asked him if he'd like to come along; he declined, as I'd hoped he would. He needs his friends.

I did feel my first wave of almost-despair, a sort of black abyss of need for Jim. Only his daddy could really comfort Jeff and meet his needs at this moment. I desperately wanted Jim to step in and help me. The first of many such moments, I fear. *I know the Lord can comfort the children, even better than we, but my feelings aren't in rhythm with that knowledge. I can see I will be learning a lot.*

Tonight's funeral service was quite different from the Episcopal service in Austin. Held in the church Jim and John and Cindi attended during their growing-up years, this service reflected John's hours of planning and preparation. I am grateful for his pastor's touch and experience.

Nearly sixteen years ago we stood before the congregation in this very church to be commissioned—sent out with their blessing— to work with InterVarsity Christian Fellowship. Wonderful years of ministry with students, part of a fellowship-family of workers committed to strengthening the kingdom. And so many of them here tonight. . . .

After the service we gathered in the church basement. Genuine friends, loving arms, some tears. But mostly I feel composed when I'm around people, perhaps because I enjoy and appreciate them so, and I don't want to stand blubbering in a corner. It's not fear of showing my weakness and vulnerability, nor is it pretense—I truly am enjoying our friends. It's been hard to make myself go and rest because I'm afraid I might miss something.

Someone said to me, "God must have known he could trust you with this." The loss, yes, but I'm afraid of the responsibility for the children's well-being. I have an overwhelming sense of inadequacy.

The under-forty members of our clan gathered later at a friend's home: my five siblings, their four spouses and assorted children, Jim's brother and sister. Some tears, lots of laughter and even more interruptions. Children were in and out, a brand-new niece was in her mother's arms: reminders of God's gifts of life and love.

I had cut a lovely daffodil from a neighbor's back yard to lay on The Box during the service. Now I want to "rescue" it from the vase on my dresser. I'm not sure why. I lay it down to die—and me to sleep.

May 5   Thursday

Morning sunshine streams onto my bed. Several friends and I are staying with the Alexanders, long-time friends and mentors in InterVarsity. This is a wonderful place to be: cozy places to talk, an atmosphere of quiet, simple elegance. I feel gently cared for but not fussed over. The small touches reveal the Alexanders' good taste: lovely breakfast china, interesting teapots, attractively presented food. And in the early mornings as I lie in bed writing in my journal, I hear a quiet stirring outside my door: Dr. Alexander has brought a tea tray, lovingly prepared. Somehow it matters that it's a china cup and silver spoon, a fabric napkin. It might have been styrofoam and plastic and paper. I sense a healing power in beauty.

Tim was right, I needed these days away. Long walks in the spring sunshine, past beds of crocuses and emerging daffodils, shrubs and trees bursting their buds—the damp, fresh smell of new life. I do miss the more defined seasons of the north. My best friend, Bonnie, has come from Michigan to be with me; I delight in the ease of our communication. Words are spoken and understood. A rare gift, even between friends.

Lin has asked if she may continue to live with us next year. *May you? Won't you? Please?* Bonnie is also considering the possibility of returning to Austin to live with our family again. It's terribly appealing to me, but somehow I have that underlying thought that I mustn't allow myself the luxury of the help and companionship of such good friends. *I should have to struggle through the aloneness as every other widow does.* But then our family has always had unique living arrangements; the unusual is ordinary for us. A graduate student from Lebanon, a variety of InterVarsity student leaders and staff workers, a succession of young working women, five different Mainland Chinese students—*what a wonderfully large and loving family we've had!*

I have been pampered this week: back rubs, bubble baths, sitting by the fireplace in a warm shawl. Last night I browsed through the early chapters of several "how to be a widow" books which Mrs. Alexander is reading to help her daughter Lynne. Heading for the tub, book in hand, I thought: *Widow, that's what I am. Guess I might as well get on with it.* But my reaction to the books was, *This isn't me, at least not now.* I don't mean I'm denying that I'm a widow, but that the "feelings which are natural" aren't a part of my experience—yet. I expect to be dealing with anger toward God and the drunk driver, frustration over finances, difficulties with the children, but I couldn't relate to the guilt part. That initial sense of completedness persists. I wonder if my grieving will be "cleaner" somehow than if we'd had a less healthy marriage. Sadness and loss, yes, but no if-only's. Perhaps those will come too. . . .

My tears seem to come in small doses—no longer floods but trickles—triggered by specific memories or thoughts or conversation. I sometimes feel, especially when I'm alone, that I could perpetuate the tearfulness with a little effort, but it seems unnecessary. I want to grieve adequately; *part of my need to do it right.* It's maybe related to my inability to concentrate, but it feels like my brain short-circuits on certain topics, and I find myself unable to pursue the worrisome "what-ifs" of our future. *That's so unlike me. I'm usually great at futile, anticipatory worrying. Could this be God's protective mechanism to keep me from the brink of total despair?*

This has been a wonderfully restful, restorative time—and place—for me: protected, sheltered, full of beauty and love. I'm surprised at my growing sense of excitement and even anticipation at the adventure ahead. While I am aware that there surely will be places of fear and despair, I'm confident that I am ultimately secure.

I recall the initial dialogue that precedes the climb up a mountain. The mountaineer above calls down to indicate that he has me securely tied into the safety system of belay ropes; I gather my courage and shout the response, indicating that I'm prepared to trust him with my life:

"On belay."

"Climbing!"

But now it really feels like it's time to go back to the reality of grief-work: sorting/giving/storing Jim's things, learning to manage a home and family without him. Even my list-making urges are returning. *Remember, he won't be there when you get home. And he's never coming back again.*

III

May 8   Sunday

One of my major tasks this week is to find a therapist for the whole family. I have arranged preliminary interviews with several psychologists whom friends have recommended. I wonder if finding the right family therapist isn't a lot like choosing a new pair of shoes: Which best suits my needs? Which feels most comfortable? And then the clincher: Can I afford this? In this case, can I afford not to do it? Even though it won't be covered by insurance, I'm convinced that this is an important investment in my family's mental health. Some things are worth the price.

Last week Ethan's nursery-school teacher reminded the children to invite their families to the spring picnic. "I think I'll ask God to let my daddy come back for that." *So this is what* the books mean: "Young children can't understand the irreversibility of death."

This afternoon, without even thinking about it, I got in the car and drove off to visit Pete in the hospital. As I climbed out of the car I realized that this was my first time as driver since Jim's death. I forgot to be afraid. I had anticipated that first venture in the car to be momentous, to find myself with an extreme attack of No Confidence.

I visited briefly with Pete, a bit taken aback by the seriousness of his injuries: traction, bandages, cuts and bruises. *Why am I surprised? And why is it so unnerving? Because I can't help thinking, if Pete looks this bad and survived, how must it have been for you, My Love?*

Jessie, with bedtime's usual tears: "I miss my daddy so much." A frequent refrain, and very healthy, I think. Then: "But I feel so sorry for that other driver. To live the rest of your life knowing that you had killed somebody's daddy and badly hurt another man—that would be a terrible thing." In her prayers: "Lord, remember that thief on the cross and how he repented and went to heaven? I hope that Mr. B will feel sorry and come to know you too." *Thank you, Lord, for my children.*

May 10   Tuesday

A quote attributed to a major fashion designer: "Women are most fascinating between the ages of thirty-five and forty, after they have run a few races and know how to pace them-

selves. Since few women ever pass forty, maximum fascination can continue indefinitely." *Now isn't that reassuring?* Yes,
I think about men in my life, and about remarriage. I was able
to think and talk about it within a few days of Jim's death.
I'm confident that wanting to marry again is a reflection of
what a fulfilling experience it was the first time. *But how much
of my eagerness is related to my lack of confidence about coping
alone? Am I just wanting someone to rescue me?*

I registered Ethan to begin kindergarten next year. Most
"first times" have not been particularly difficult for me, but
writing *Deceased* in the father/husband blank did give me
pause.

I'm surprised at my usual composure; others seem to be too.
I'm not really working at it—if the tears are there, I let them
come. It sometimes seems I should be feeling a much heavier
weight of grief. I hope I'm not pushing it off, to have to suffer
more later. I am trying to grieve thoroughly; I'd prefer to do
a good job the first time and not have to redo parts of it. *Is
efficiency my highest aim? Remember when one of the students
who lived with us left a message for me on the refrigerator with
the kids' magnetic alphabet letters? "Efficiency is next to godliness."*

Mom has stayed on a few more days to help with household chores while I begin to sort and move Jim's things. *Since
I have to live in this room alone, I might as well make space for
my stuff. If I ever marry again I hope he doesn't need more than
two drawers.* I find this task exhausting. Everything I pick up
requires a decision: Will one of the children want this someday? Shall I save it? give it away? Who could use it? Who
might it fit? I don't want to get rid of things I may someday

wish I'd kept. But I'm also convinced that things are to be used and enjoyed, not stored forever and ever. I'm pulled between the practical and the sentimental.

My work is interspersed with regular weeping sessions and trips to the tissue box as I come across unexpected "treasures": a neckerchief slide Jim made during his Boy Scout years. Rainbow-striped suspenders for his sillier moods. The journal he kept while on a month-long Outward Bound trip, including a letter from me in which I had tucked a picture of six-month-old Jeffrey smiling for his daddy. The .22 rifle he bought for me during our poverty-stricken first year of marriage—I had found it standing in the kitchen sink tied with a large yellow bow.

His clothes: the favorite shirts, tweedy sport coats, the down vest we'd made together from a kit. And all the "toys" which reflected his wide variety of interests: archery equipment, art supplies, fly-tying and fishing paraphernalia, hand-crafted knives in various stages of completion, beginner's taxidermy supplies. What should I do with his razor and shaving mug? his aftershave lotions and talc? *Why does the sense of smell trigger such powerful emotions?*

I work a bit and then sit or lie down to rest, ofttimes to cry. It isn't the quantity of stuff, but rather the nature of the experience that makes the task seem interminable. *Should this small part of the one I loved most dearly go into this box or that one?* Sighs, tears, smiles and even laughter, sighs, more sighs. The sighs have come to indicate "overload" to me, time to stop and rest, to try deliberately to release my body's tension.

While I still need to rest frequently throughout the day, I

find that some of the very physical symptoms of those first days are diminishing: extreme shortness of breath, that choking sensation, involuntary moans, the bone-weary feeling that my whole body is made of lead, a dry mouth, heart palpitations.

There is still the stabbing, piercing pain as the realization that Jim is indeed gone sweeps over me again and again. I sometimes find myself moving about as though I am enshrouded in a thin casing of ice, like a sapling after a winter storm. *Fragile. If I move suddenly or in the wrong way, I will shatter. And then, like Humpty Dumpty, who could put me together again?*

May 11   Wednesday

This afternoon I took Jeff out to buy sneakers. I asked him to help me select stationery for thank-you notes, and then we went to the hospital. Jeff didn't say much, but Pete seemed glad to see him.

Later we checked the oil in the old blue Volvo and added water to the radiator. *Wasn't it just three weeks ago that Jim pointed out to me some of the idiosyncrasies of this engine?*

Jeff came in tonight for a few minutes and cried on my pillow. He has beautiful eyes; when bright with tears, they become almost turquoise. *These kids all got their daddy's beautiful long eyelashes. I remember when Jessie was a button-nosed toddler having her profile "snipped" by a silhouette artist. Stopping* in mid-snip she looked up and said, "Do you realize this child's eyelashes extend further than her nose?"

When he cries, Jeff kind of scrunches up his face and squeezes out the tears. I asked him to try to tell me what he was thinking, but he says it just hurts more. Earlier when I mentioned our going to a counselor sometime, he didn't want to discuss it; he just shook his head no. He really needs to verbalize his feelings. Maybe what I mean is, it helps *me* when I do that.

I wondered if seeing Pete's bruises and cuts and casts and traction prompted Jeff to wonder how it was for Daddy. When I asked, he said yes. How can I help him tell me without "leading the witness"?

May 13   Friday

Lin and I talked this morning about the photographs which a friend sent of the wrecked cars. I don't have the whatever-it-takes to look at them just yet. The sheriff's report indicated that Pete had driven far off the road to avoid the oncoming car. The angle of the crash meant that the driver's side took the worst of the impact. Lin says it's amazing that Pete ever survived, judging from the condition of the car. In contrast, Jim's seat was almost undamaged, and the sheriff said they were both wearing seat belts. Yet that narrow strip of metal from the windshield penetrated just below Jim's browline and killed him almost instantly. *How precise.* A few inches in another direction, a few moments longer at the stoplight three miles back, different speeds, different angles might have made a difference. My sense of confidence in God's control of details is strong and inexplicable. I don't know why he wanted Jim to come "home" right now, but if it had to be, I'm glad it was so precise. No lingering comas, hospital bills, difficult life-sustaining decisions. *A sudden blow for both of us, but quick, clean, decisive.*

There are times when I feel a touch of melodrama, a sensation of stepping out of our situation and looking at it from an observer's eyes: I am appalled. *How can she possibly cope? A phone call in the night, three children, family far away.* But the realities of living this out usually feel quite different: an almost constant sense of God's comfort, a feeling of being enfolded in his arms, gently carried; friends pouring out their love in practical ways; gratitude for Jim's foresight in providing for us legally and financially; a strong sense of the rightness of God's timing.

So many illustrations of God's perfect timing come to mind. Ever since our move to Texas eight years ago we had been trying to get a satisfactory family picture. It finally happened last month; Jim and I selected the finished portrait just days before his death. Fresh from the photographer, the smiling family of five on the mantel observes the traumatic transition.

And Lin's back surgery, originally planned for this week, had had to be rescheduled when she re-injured her back last month. As a result she'd had surgery just two weeks before Jim's death. After a few days in the hospital we moved her home, putting her on the sofa so we could more easily attend to her needs. Those first days she measured her off-the-bed time in minutes, and a walk around the block was a major accomplishment. Yet Tim, her surgeon, pronounced her well enough to accompany me to Madison for the funeral.

His ways are not our ways, nor his thoughts our thoughts. . . .

May 14   Saturday

A musical ice cream truck came down our street the other evening, and Grandpa treated the kids and their flock of neighborhood friends. Tonight we heard it coming again— at bedtime. I said no, but I heard Ethan's little feet flying down the stairs, across the living room, out the front door. I scooped him up just as he started down the porch steps. A brief protest, and then he lay in my arms, sobbing. *These tears have nothing to do with ice cream.* I think he weeps for a daddy lost, something I haven't seen him really do until now. Displaced grief. If I find myself doing that occasionally with my anger I shouldn't be surprised to see him do it with his tears.

May 16   Monday

Our contractor friend came by today to discuss installing the new kitchen window. Jim and I had selected it just days before he died; it was delivered the day after the funeral. *It can stand here in the garage forever (or until it gets broken), or I can just go on and have it installed. I'm a big girl now.* When we went on to discuss the bill he said, "Now don't fuss at me, but I want to do this as a gift for you and Jim." *My God, you have given me such wonderful friends.*

Charlie came by to return the clothes he couldn't use. He was wearing one of Jim's shirts. *It seems strange to hug Jim's shirt on another man's body.* I felt a decided pang, but I'm pleased that his clothes can be useful.

Sometimes I feel like advertising that I will be taking applications soon for the position of father/husband—"Send résumés and recommendations." *It will take a special kind of man to want to take on a widow and three children . . . but then I'm not looking for an ordinary man.* I feel mostly confident that he is out there somewhere and will eventually turn up. But I have occasional flashes of fear that God may leave me single. *Why do we react that way, thinking that just because we really want something, God won't let us have it? Doesn't that reflect a distorted view of God's character? And why do I find the prospect of long-term singleness so frightening?* It's sometimes harder to deal with the what-ifs of the future than with the real circumstances in which he leads me.

When I first heard Ethan say, "I wish I could die so I could be with my daddy," I tended not to take it too seriously. But after several more reports of it, I decide to speak firmly to this. "It wouldn't make your daddy happy. And it would make us very, very sad."

I'm in bed tonight before seven, a frustratingly helpless, dependent kind of fatigue. Even though I had read a lot about

the grieving process, I'm continually surprised by the physical
exhaustion that accompanies this experience for me. For several days my afternoon rests haven't yielded sleep, and last
night my bedtime was sabotaged by unexpected guests. Today, against my better judgment, I skipped my afternoon nap
to go somewhere with a friend. It was fun, but now I pay. . . .
I'm acutely aware of my emotional fragility when I haven't had
enough sleep. By supper time I was weeping in my soup; so
Lin sent me to bed. I felt bad leaving it all to Lin as she was
also overtired, but she insisted. *Bless her. What would I do
without her?*

I am again waking too early in the morning and dozing
fitfully until the alarm tells me it's time to get the troops roused
for school. Plus Ethan has been "checking in" at some point
nearly every night, so I have to take him back to his own bed.

Tonight I take the second sleeping pill of my life.

May 17 *Tuesday*

Aftereffects of that sleeping pill kept me from driving today. A disconnected sort of feeling, out of balance. Hard rain
today; heavy storms last night.

May 19   Thursday

A friend came by after lunch. I think it's become her Thursday ritual: a warm hug, a few words and a lovely single flower. Today it was a stem of lily-of-the-valley in a tiny cylindrical vase. *One of my favorite flowers, delicate and fragrant; it used to carpet a shaded corner of our garden in Michigan.* Nancy remembers that Thursday noon was the last time I saw Jim. *In all the years of your traveling, Jim, we'd had a lot of practice in your comings and goings. We said our usual, casual good-bys that day. And I fully expected to wake up with you beside me. What was it you said? "I'll be home around one." Yes, you were Home— but not on Woodrow Street.*

IV

T his afternoon Jessie played Annie in the musical produc-
tion put on by her gifted music class. As I entered the school
auditorium I looked over the cast seated in the front row, but
couldn't find her. In her bright curly red wig and exaggerated
freckles, she seemed like a different person! She looked so
cute and did very well playing her part. Predictably, I wished
Jim could be here. I cried a bit as I adopted the "bystander"
position again: *And to think this child just lost her daddy three
weeks ago! What a kid!*

   We all went to Bill and Carolyn's for supper tonight. A
pasta-making party: mild chaos with six kids, but lots of fun
and very tasty. Keeping the little guys from tangling themselves in the yards of pasta draped across the backs of the

kitchen chairs kept several of us busy. As I walked through the kitchen, plates in hand, I suddenly crumbled. All the good times we've had over the years with these friends—*it just doesn't seem right that Jim isn't here. How many thousands of times will I hear those words in my head over the next days, weeks, months, years?*

May 22   Sunday

We took our first out-of-town excursion today: a sixty-mile drive to see Aunt Eylene, our only Texas relative. Jeff had spent last night at a friend's house. ("Sleeping over" is only half-correct: lots of "over," not much sleeping.) He napped both coming and going, and most of the time we were there; the rest of the time he was rather surly. About forty minutes out of Austin, Lin and I panicked when the red AMP light flashed on. It stayed on, even though the car continued to roll right along. We stopped at an unhelpful filling station; I was afraid to turn the car off for fear it wouldn't start again. We proceeded on. *Am I ruining this car by continuing to drive it?* Later, from Aunt Eylene's we called another station. Mechanics and garages are nonexistent on Sundays, but someone suggested it might be a fuse. *A fuse! Of course! Why didn't I think of that? Life is so simple when you know what you're doing.*

May 24   Tuesday

Had lunch today with a friend who has been divorced for some time; over dessert we discussed my re-entry into the world of men and dating after more than sixteen years. In a "don't be too naive" voice she warned, "The world isn't populated with Jim Wordens, you know." *Don't I know it. And I vacillate between adolescent eagerness and sheer terror. Am I ready for this?*

Collected conversations with Jessie: "I don't see why God didn't at least give Daddy a chance to live. Even if he had two broken legs, sure, he'd be different, but at least we'd still have him." "You and Daddy always told us 'life isn't fair' but I thought you just said that so I wouldn't feel bad when I couldn't stay over at a friend's house." "Yes, sometimes I feel a little angry at God, but I know he still loves me even if I say that." She is able to speak her anger, but tentatively and with qualifiers.

May 27   Friday

No school today—I can sleep in. Or at least I can stay in bed.

May 28   Saturday

A major confrontation with Jeff today. A series of "misun-derstandings" accumulated, until it finally dawned on me that they really all translated into "disobedience." The showdown came when I had to cancel his plans to sleep at Ben's at the last moment. A very sullen boy dragged his sleeping bag into the back of the station wagon. When we got home, he dis-appeared. Some mysterious thumps led me to the attic where he was digging through the camping gear. As I came up the ladder he looked at me, backpack in hand, "I'm leaving." "You can't! And besides, that's *my* new backpack." *But I can't stop him. He's just as big as I am.* Then I crumbled; I felt so aban-doned. . . . We sat on the floor and cried together and I told him how much I needed to be able to trust him, for him to be obedient. More tears. While Lin took care of the others, Jeff and I sat on my bed and ate our raspberry yogurt together, and then played cards. *Another high hurdle crossed. I'm not certain that we left it upright, but at least we're still moving on— on toward the next one.*

May 30   Monday

Another good friend has come for a few days. Dave came to the funeral; I'm glad Diane waited until after the intensity of those days for an extended visit. And it's good of Dave to send her off while he stays with their four children.

I like the growing awareness of this new generation of fathers about the importance of their role in parenting. I love to see daddies pushing strollers, or playing with their kids in the park, or taking them to the library. Jim had always held a decidedly liberated view of fathering. The flexibility of his job schedule allowed him to sometimes walk them to school or join them for lunch in the cafeteria; when he was in town he could attend their awards assemblies and even take his turn at being the "helping mother" in their nursery schools. Does this make our loss even greater? I wonder if the intensity of the relationship dictates the depth of pain felt at its absence? *How is it for you, children? It's impossible for me to really know. I lost my husband. You lost your daddy. It doesn't necessarily translate.*

Yesterday I took Diane to brunch at Green Pastures, an old plantation-house-turned-restaurant. Peacocks on the lawn, pink linen tablecloths, silver flatware, waiters refolding your napkin every time you go to one of the various buffet tables, unobtrusive piano music, milk punch—elegance of another era. We spent the afternoon in quiet conversation, reveling in the ambience. *How does that verse go? "Health for the body and food for the soul. . . ."*

As I venture out in new roles, I find a slowly growing self-confidence: making reservations, selecting a table, paying the bill, driving to and from the myriad destinations I now have. *Sometimes I still forget and head for the passenger door of the car.* I have lived a rather protected life, and I guess I pretty much liked it that way. Suddenly I have no choice. Or, looked at another way, my choices are almost limitless.

May 31   Tuesday

Tonight Lin and Diane and I listened to the tape someone thoughtfully recorded of the first funeral. Sadness. And hope. In spite of my apprehensions, the service more than met my expectations. *I was so afraid it wouldn't adequately reflect you, Jim, and your flair for "doing it right," with simplicity, even elegance. But it did. I wish you could have been there beside us. You would have loved it.*

A phrase from one of the prayers caught me: "Jim, laying his standard before the Lord, the Holy One." It draws pictures in my mind. I can almost see him, "Here I am, Lord, reporting in."

And here's a job for him. The other day Jessie said, "I think I'll ask God to let Daddy be my guardian angel." Someone said to me: "Wow! Will he be busy. That's a bigger job than he ever had down here." *Jessie, you're a treasure.*

Tonight I begin the process of reading through the letters Jim wrote to me during our four years of long-distance courtship. I tuck myself into bed, letters on one side and a box of tissues on the other. . . .

June 2   Thursday

I still struggle to grip the reality of our loss. Images associated with his death (the smashed cars, his head injury, cremation) or of his presence elsewhere (worshiping the Lord in a new way) are vivid, but only fleeting. My mind shifts almost immediately to coping with life's everyday details, getting on with our lives. I'm not sure that's all good. Somewhere, lurking in the back of my brain, is the half-expectation that Jim will step back into my life, will commend me for handling things so well. "See, I knew you could do it." *Why do I still have such a great need for your approval and affirmation, Jim?*

When I started seeing the counselor, I discussed with him my seemingly urgent need to order my life, to get on immediately with the tasks of sorting, cleaning out, giving away. He pointed out that for a person who values order and predictability, the unexpected death of a loved one is the epitome of loss of control. These are my small attempts to convince myself that I'm in charge of my life, our lives. I am, like it or not, responsible; but in a bigger sense I'm not ultimately in control. There's something reassuring about that.

More bedtime reading of Jim's letters: sadness and joy. Bittersweet.

June 3   Friday

I want to send a "report" to our many friends, but I had despaired of ever being able to communicate some of what we'd been learning in these difficult days of our lives. I woke from my nap today with phrases for the letter I'd been hoping to produce hanging in my mind, dangling from slender threads. Without rolling over I groped for my ever-present pen. *If I move, the threads will snap, those just-right words lost to me forever.* I scribbled them on the backs of envelopes from the mail I'd opened before I went to sleep. *At last! That letter may become a reality after all.* I write, almost desperately, afraid I will lose the words or be interrupted. I find out later that Lin, having peeked in to be sure I was still breathing, threatened to string the kids up by their thumbs if they interrupt me. I finally emerged, scribbles on scraps, triumphant.

Triumph, then tears. From the high life of Green Pastures to the low-life reality of lice. Examining Ethan's itchy head we find one or two of the little beasties and their accompanying egg cases, called nits. Looking like a tiny grain of salt, they can only be removed by sliding them individually off the hair shaft. "Nit-picking"—that's what those monkeys are doing to each other at the zoo. The special shampoo, a syrupy, smelly and toxic treatment, must be applied to the dry hair and smooshed around. *If he has it, and the neighbor kid has it, should I shampoo Jeff? and Jessie? myself? Lin? How many nights did I snuggle beside him on his pillow?*

We strip his bed, washing everything in hot water and

bleach. *How many beds should I do? Jim, why are you not here when I need you?* As a three-time mother I know this is one of the Common Communicable Diseases of Childhood, but still I feel paranoid, as if we've been invaded. *Someday, Lord, you're going to have some questions to answer. And my list is growing longer. Why ever did you create lice? And while we're at it, what about those cockroaches?*

June 5   Sunday

Had a few bad moments as I drove home today: I glanced into my rearview mirror, alerted by the sound of screeching tires and brakes. I saw the cars careen, and crash. The sight and sound sickened me. Assured that no one was hurt, I drove on for a few blocks. As I stepped out of the car, I was overcome with weakness and shaking. How wonderful to have a friend there to hold me until the moment passed.

Tonight Ethan asked if we could adopt a new daddy. And if so, "Could we still be our whole family, even Auntie Lin?" When I asked how we might do that he said, "I guess we just look for one—one who doesn't already have a momma." He assured me they would all help look. When he approached the others about it, Jeff replied, "Just make sure he hunts." And Jessie, with her usual candor, responded, "I don't want a new daddy, and I don't want to talk about it."

Next week I'm going to Colorado for a week to visit friends—and to scatter some of Jim's ashes at two of our favorite places. I'm a bit reluctant about leaving the kids, but I know they'll be fine under Lin's care. And I feel an inner urging to begin my pilgrimage, returning to those places which held so much importance in my life with Jim. When I chose cremation I vaguely realized that I would have to decide whether to bury or store the ashes, or scatter them.

It occurred to me much later that I actually had several compatible options. Later this summer we plan to have a burial service in the family cemetery plot in Wisconsin. His parents will appreciate having a place they can return to. But I've also planned to take out a small portion of the ashes to scatter at four special places: a favorite mountain lake in Colorado, the base of the rock where I had my first rock-climbing experience, the place in Michigan where I first met Jim and a favorite waterfowl marsh on my father's property.

My original decision for cremation was based on pragmatic considerations. Now I realize the additional benefits: weeks and months later we're emotionally more able to process the disposal of the ashes. I think this gives us an advantage over having to complete all the important rituals in those first few days. I've never been very tolerant of the trappings that ac-company the usual burials, and in this case we can do it completely on our own.

At Bill's urging I took out an insurance policy on myself last week. I was surprised to discover how inexpensively I could get considerable coverage with term insurance. The thought of my children being doubly orphaned is too much for me to grasp. But at least they wouldn't be a financial burden to their guardians.

June 8   Wednesday

Another good friend has waited to come and will spend this next week with us. Marcia is a "craftsy" person and has offered to do some sewing projects for me. We went out for lunch, then checked a number of stores to find the supplies we needed. Taking my check and asking for more than the usual identification, the saleswoman asked for my work number. Getting a blank look she then asked, "Your husband's work number?" I hesitated, and she said impatiently, "Well, where does he work?" I couldn't resist a smile, though I stifled the obvious but flippant response. *She must be new at this. So am I.*

We trekked on, stopping at the grocery for the inevitable two gallons of milk and loaf of bread. I was very weary by now, my "togetherness" sliding away. I wrote the check and started to walk off, forgetting to give it to the cashier. *I shouldn't have skipped that nap.*

June 9   Thursday

As I walked out of Ethan's room at bedtime he said, "Can't we talk some about Daddy tonight?" I turned back to him and he said, "Not our daddy who died, but the new one we're looking for." So we talked about the qualities that were important to us. "Does it matter if he's tall or short? kind or gentle? dark hair or light? if he knows Jesus or not?"

Ethan had asked me this afternoon about finding a new daddy, suggesting that he could help. When I asked how we should do that he replied thoughtfully, "Well, just line up a whole bunch of boys and then pick one—but pick a skinny one!"

June 10   Friday

There is so much to do before we leave to spend the summer in Michigan, especially since I will be gone for a week in Colorado. I need to think of things I can ask others to do for us, turning their general offers of help into specific requests. It isn't hard for me to accept help, especially when I'm desperate. But anticipating my needs and recruiting help when I feel good is much more difficult.

June 11   Saturday

Why did the other driver, Mr. B (who had a DWI record "as long as your arm" according to the sheriff), survive instead of Jim, a "productive man of God"? Perhaps to allow Mr. B another opportunity to make different choices for his life— and possibly for eternity? Here's his "second chance." I'd like to meet him someday and try to communicate some of that to him. I'd also like Mr. B to know that the children and I pray for him. We agreed to use his name; it somehow seems contradictory to pray for "that man" or "the other driver."

I asked Lin to separate out some of Jim's ashes for me; I just couldn't face doing it by myself. Dilemma: What kind of containers? *I know how aesthetically offended you were by Tupperware. I can't do that to you, even now.* Lin and Charles finally decided on Ziploc plastic bags. As they handed me the small, but surprisingly heavy, carefully wrapped package: "There's something we think you should know. This is not just finely powdered ash; it's sort of . . . 'chunky,' with bone fragments." My heart sinks, struck again by hard reality.

V

Soft white feathers of snow have been falling all night; the deck has four or five inches of fluff. The trees are all powdered. The world is clean and quiet, muffled. If this is June, this can't be Texas.

I arrived in Denver on Saturday. Tim, a friend from our student summer projects of several years ago, met me at the airport. As we drove to Breckenridge we talked about Jim, about Tim's deep respect and love for him. Two summers of working together in ministry had forged a strong bond between them.

I'm staying with John and Carrie, friends from those special summers. Their home is a quiet, restful place. They own a clothing store together with Tim, and they have arranged for me to come in later today for a "shopping spree." What a wonderful gift—and timely, since I'm down at least ten pounds from my usual weight and none of my clothes fit.

I sat reading in the sun, the snow melting. I looked back over my underlinings in the book I had begun reading before Jim died.

Nothing counts more in the way we live than what we believe about God. A failure to get it right in our minds becomes a failure to get it right in our lives. . . .

None of the things we fear or suffer are untrue, but none has the power to center our lives, or dominate our emotions, or control our destiny. God does that. . . .

We have been bullied by our emotions into concluding that if we don't feel happy something is wrong at the core of the universe, that if we don't have what we want when we want it, then we are being deprived of our rights, that if we are suffering or feeling pain then God is not doing his job. [Eugene Peterson, *Traveling Light*, IVP, pp. 34-35, 38, 51.]

Tonight a group of friends came for supper, and afterwards we listened to the tape of the Austin funeral. We followed the liturgy in the Book of Common Prayer, sang the hymns and wept together. They had loved Jim too; this was their memorial service for him.

He has sent me to bind up the brokenhearted . . . to comfort all who mourn, and provide for those who grieve . . . to bestow on them a crown of beauty instead of ashes, the oil of gladness instead of mourning, and a garment of praise instead of a spirit of despair. They will be called oaks of righteousness, a planting of the LORD for the display of his splendor. (Is 61:1-3)

June 14   Tuesday

Today I did one of the most difficult things of my thirty-six years, second only to telling the children that their daddy was never coming home again. After lunch Tim and I walked down to the lake where I was to scatter Jim's ashes.

As we walked down the mountain road my mind screamed, *How can I do this?* And I asked God for the strength I didn't feel. We were there. Goose Pasture Tarn. Memories. *. . . The many early-morning fishing trips you enjoyed here. The smell and taste of fresh-caught trout frying for breakfast. The day we two spent floating aimlessly on this little lake, talking and laughing. It was my birthday, and you had packed a lovely lunch, complete with a pillowcase-covered board as a table over the gunnels, a pair of wine glasses. And fabric napkins. Even the afternoon squall didn't spoil our day. We just held the tarp over our heads, letting the canoe drift and listening to the raindrops. And the almost unbelievable rainbow we saw as we left town that last day of our second summer—one end in the lake and the other on shore. It seemed to vibrate with brightness and promise.*

The mountain lake sparkled like jewels. The day was crystal clear and lovely, but I felt surrounded by dark clouds. I put my hand into the ashes and I sprinkled them over the water. A light breeze blew some of the powder back on me. Conspicuous white fragments lay on the bottom as the floating ash moved away. I finished and the wrenching sobs began. Tim stooped to put his arm around me; I wept on his knees.

Before we left I rolled down my cuffs, brushing the residue off my pant legs and jacket. We turned to go back up the hill. As I moistened my dry lips, I noticed an acrid taste on my tongue; it took a moment for me to realize what it was.

June 15   Wednesday

I spent the morning rather meditatively. Lying on the couch with the tissue box, salt trails on my face, and tears in my ears, I missed Jim desperately—his physical presence—and my whole body ached to be caressed.

In the afternoon I walked through the village, along familiar streets and paths. The downtown shops, the grocery store and library, the church where we had worshiped together, and the condominiums where we had spent such wonderful months as a family. We enjoyed using our home as a gathering place for students during the two summers that Jim directed the Breckenridge Evangelism Project. Buffet suppers, popcorn and TV movies, worship times, Sunday brunches, quiet conversations over tea and cookies. I stop for a few minutes outside our condo, The Cedars #19. I walk across the bridge, listening to the creek and noticing "Ethan's rock," where as a three-year-old Ethan had liked to spend meditative moments just watching the water go by. I look up at our front porch, the balcony, our bedroom window. I feel immersed in pain, as close as I've come to real despair. *God, what we had was so good! Now how are you ever going to fix this?*

I walk back to sit in the sunshine, to cry my tears and my agony out to God. Tim slips into the chair beside me and takes my hand. He listens. And he knows he doesn't have to defend God. He's a true friend. *I feel terribly sad; my heart is broken, and I fear I will never be happy again.*

June 16   Thursday   *Bear Trap Ranch, Colorado*

A brief visit to Bear Trap Ranch, another place of many memories. One of InterVarsity's student training centers, this tiny valley nestled high in the peaks above Colorado Springs had been a delightful home for our family on a number of occasions. Month-long summer discipleship camps, holiday houseparties for international students at Christmas time. We had all thrived on the clear mountain air and bright sunshine. *Cozy* was a good word for the cabins (some might have said *cramped*). Rustic old log cabins with sloping ceilings and tiny windows are charming, but a little tight with all five of us in one room when the camp was full.

In spite of my hesitation, Jim had accepted the invitation to become the director of the Ranch. ("Why ever would you want to add a third management position to your already overbusy life?" "Because I think it might tap into my creative juices in a way which I could really enjoy.") He was quite right.

He had delighted in poring over blueprints and discussing with the architect the plans for the new building, a huge log structure to provide housing for staff and families. Last summer the foundation had been poured, and construction had begun in earnest. The massive logs were each scribed and hand cut to fit together, then swung into place by a special block-and-tackle system rigged on the "gin pole," a sixty-foot lodgepole pine which had been secured in the center of the foundation.

Jim had visited the Ranch just a month before he died, and he returned with enthusiastic reports about the project. Seeing it now, the massive log frame with the beginnings of a roof, I was awed. And a tour of the interior left me marveling at the craftsmanship and loving care with which the work had been done.

As manager of Bear Trap, Dave had shared Jim's apprehension about the possible damage their friendship might suffer with Jim's appointment as director of the Ranch, making him Dave's supervisor. But instead their respect for one another had grown and their friendship had thrived. Without a doubt those hunting trips arranged to coincide with Jim's "supervisory visits" had been profitable in a number of ways. Now a wonderful friendship was lost. How varied are the griefs suffered by those whose lives touch ours.

Dave and Tim walked with me up the mountainside to the base of the rock formation which had so challenged (let's speak the truth: terrified) me last summer. I am now so grateful for that experience, learning that I could do what at first looked to be impossible. *Take a few deep breaths, listen to the encouragement of friends, trust yourself to the belay line. You're securely roped in to the mountaineering instructor; he's been this way before with many others. You may be frightened, you may even slip, but you won't fall very far. You're safe; you're on belay.* The powerful image, which came after the phone call, of the new and unexpected mountain prompted me to choose this place to scatter some of Jim's ashes. *Frightened, but ultimately secure. "On belay." "Climbing!"*

June 17   Friday   *Colorado Springs*

Sixteen years ago today I was a bride.

As I took my walk this morning in the Garden of the Gods, I remembered that our wedding day was a day like this, clear and sunny—but in the very different setting of northern Michigan. Two weeks of rain had left the world lush and green (soggy?) and had convinced my mother to consider alternatives to the back-yard reception. Dad and I, however, were unwavering in our conviction that it couldn't possibly rain on my reception. We were right, even if everyone's shoes were a little muddy. *Our friend Dick, playing the cello under that clump of white birch trees. The wedding cake, so beautifully decorated by your mother with some help from our sisters. . . . And that morning in the upstairs bedroom our three grandmothers sat chatting together while they wrapped pieces of groom's cake for the guests. A lovely, wonderful, long-awaited day of celebration. And at last, after four years of correspondence, telephone calls and painful partings, I could finally sit beside you in "our car." As we drove off together I remember thinking, "Now we will never have to say good-by again." How wrong I was.*

VI

Flying home, I reflected on my pilgrimage back to Colorado. Favorite places, fine friends—I only wish I could have
had more time with each of them. Contrary to my original
plans, I spent most of my time in Breckenridge. But I will
return to the Ranch, to walk the paths, recall the memories,
indulge the tears. Better, I think, to have "done" one well and
be returning home rested.

The flight into Austin from the west is spectacular. I am
caught by its beauty: the meandering river, dammed into
several lakes; rugged hills, green with mesquite and cedar; the
city sprawling into the hill country. We had never expected
Texas to be like this and hadn't planned to stay more than
three years. But Austin has been a very good place for us: a

lovely old house in a friendly neighborhood, a good church home, supportive and loving friends. *I'm so glad our parents were there to see the lavish support and care of our friends. No one has ever hinted that perhaps we should move back North, closer to family so they can "take care of us."*

June 19   Sunday

I spent most of the day in bed, wrestling with a roaring sinus headache. Could it have something to do with this being Father's Day?

June 20   Monday

I'm trying to get back into a routine of early morning walks around the nearby golf course; I feel much better when I'm getting regular exercise. This morning as I came over the rise there was a light-colored Jeep Cherokee parked along the curb. *It looks just like the pictures of the car which hit Pete and Jim.* I indulged my irrational urge to kick a tire. Futility. Like a child beating his fists on his daddy's chest, or kicking this tire until my toes are bruised—it's a picture of my helplessness to alter the fact of our loss. *I must carefully conserve my energies, spending them like a miser on those important things which can restore health and wholeness to our family.*

Most of this day was spent struggling through the lawn mowing with Jeff and Jessie. *Wouldn't it be easier just to do it myself?* But we emerged friends, and someone else will worry about mowing it for the next two months. Somewhere under all this is an important lesson. *Yes, we can make it, but it won't be easy. And we'll have to work together.*

At several points today I felt overwhelmed by the reality of Jim's absence, a "This can't be true and it can't be happening to me" feeling. Each time it comes it seems to take a different form, all of which are pretty nearly indescribable. Have I just been numb for two months? *Have I been deep-down denying it all?* I felt engulfed in waves of tears; not despair, but heart-rending sadness. *Lord, help me to know that even while it feels worse, it's getting better. I know the pain and sadness will be at times more intense and may seem unbearable—but I also know that it can't go on forever.*

June 23   Thursday

Because I am a reluctant shopper and I enter malls only out of dire necessity, I opted for the nearby department store to find summer-camp clothes for Jeff and Jessica. That accomplished, I suddenly found myself on "automatic pilot" headed for the sales racks in the lingerie department. *Why am I doing this? Haven't I just packed away most of my lovelier and more exotic things for some hoped-for future?* Standing in the aisle between the cooking pots and the silky negligees, I determined that this will be an aspect of my life which I choose to nurture and encourage in spite of the inevitable frustration. I don't want this part of me to die with Jim; I wish very much to stay in touch with my sexuality, my femininity, my awareness of myself as a woman. Single life isn't all button-to-the-neck granny gowns, and I want my children to grow up with the understanding that our sexuality is to be valued as an important part of God's creative gift.

June 24   Friday

The kids and Lin and I are on our way to Chicago, spread out comfortably in the spacious and unoccupied "handicapped" section of the train. Our kids have always enjoyed train travel, and I certainly didn't have it in me to make this trip in our ten-year-old Volvo. (I don't think the Volvo had it either.)

The last few days of preparation have left me exhausted. Making arrangements to have someone forward the mail and care for the house and yard, packing my own things and overseeing the children's choices. . . . The myriad details finally got the better of me, and last-minute kinks in our travel plans put me over the brink; I crawled into bed last night, beaten.

Fifteen-hundred miles on the train is easy; getting from Chicago to a tiny town in northern Michigan is the tough part. When last night's eleven o'clock phone call revealed that we had no rental car reservation, my brain hit a brick wall. I have on rare occasions felt physically at the end of my tether, "Not one more step." But never, before April, had I experienced this mental/emotional overload which throws the off switch. There have been times in the last two months when, in my fatigue, I have felt unable to go an inch further in my thinking, understanding, deciding. The system simply shuts down. And last night mine did. "Lin, please do whatever you can to fix this—I just want to be somewhere other than Union Station on Saturday night." Not exactly at the peak of energy herself, still she willingly took over. *How would we manage without her?* I may have sold our souls to the rental car agency, but at least we're not hitchhiking to Carney.

June 25   Saturday   *Carney, Michigan*

I am exhausted and have been sent to bed. The children feel no weariness in their excitement at being back here again. They're all in the shower or tub—after all, it is Saturday night at Grandma's house.

June 27   Monday

Visited with Aunt Clara for a while this morning, went to Cindi's for lunch, made a quick stop at my sister's on my way home—and I felt whipped. Took a nap, but still felt weepy and vulnerable in the evening. Just "coming down" from the long trip? Or will I be this fragile and unresilient for the rest of my life?

June 28   Tuesday

Jim's birthday. It wasn't a particularly difficult day for me, but I expected it might be for his parents. I had arranged for a friend in Madison to deliver a single rose with the note: "To express our thanks for your part in making Jim the gift he was to all of us. Love, MJ, J, J, and EJ."

In the past few days I've noticed a slight change in my response to looking at Jim's picture, to thinking of his actual death. That piercing, shattering awareness of "this person no longer exists—he's never coming back" is being replaced by a dull, thudding pain; a grudging acceptance; a feeling of it becoming a part of the past, not such an immediate reality. Is that because I'm in a different setting? extra tired from travel? Or is it a new phase of grieving? In spite of the pain of acute awareness, I almost prefer that intensity of feeling to the dull ache of going on. Am I reluctant to leave the "glorious past" for the unknown future?

June 30   Thursday

T he kids are thriving here, thoroughly enjoying their many cousins and the new adventures of a rural setting: making forts in the field or horse barn, riding the three-wheelers, playing with the bunnies. The aunts have been wonderful about inviting the Texas cousins over to play, to eat over, to sleep over. In fact, I think Jeff may have moved in with Jeremy.

Some of these mornings I lie abed remembering, weeping, writing in my journal; sometimes I enjoy a brisk walk down country roads, delighting in the early summer sunshine. Today I was joined by an annoying group of buzzing flies, zinging tight circles around my head, persisting in spite of the fern I was flailing. They won; I turned back.

July 1   Friday

U p the hill, past the spacious farmhouse, down the hill, kicking the white gravel. Ahead of me the country road takes an abrupt turn, slicing through fields of hay ripening in the early summer sun. *My life feels like that—I'm about to turn a significant corner in my grieving.* It's no longer the piercing, stabbing pain of new grief, rather the pain has become more vague, a more generalized discomfort. And no more welcome for its growing familiarity.

> To thee, O LORD,
>   I lift up my soul.
> O my God, in thee I trust. . . .
> Turn thou to me, and be gracious to me;
>   for I am lonely and afflicted.
> Relieve the troubles of my heart,
>   and bring me out of my distresses.
> Consider my affliction and my trouble,
>   and forgive all my sins. . . .
> All the paths of the LORD are
>   steadfast love and faithfulness. (Ps 25 RSV)

All the paths, Lord? All the paths.

July 2 *Saturday*

Summer days full of the usual family busyness: meals, laundry, trips to town, picking strawberries, church obligations. Other people's responsibilities for the most part, so I can often withdraw, rest, take a walk or work on mailing out the letters. Adding personal notes to all two-hundred-plus copies of that letter I wrote several weeks ago may take me the entire summer; I'm only in the D's.

July 3   Sunday

Baby animals—new life. This afternoon my brother Bruce and I took his kids, mine and assorted other cousins out to a friend's farm to see the new families: ducks, turkeys, calves, pigs. Hanging over fences, gently touching and holding the babies, squealing with laughter, running through pastures, topping it all off with ice cream cones from the farmhouse kitchen—a memorable afternoon. And a fragrant ride home with someone's shoe mucky from a misstep in the barn.

As we dropped cousins off at their various homes, I over-heard Ethan say, "Julie, are you getting out here? Good. I don't like you" or something to that effect. I was crushed for her (or was it for me?). I confronted him on the spot, but of course it was too late: the words were out, and there was a limit to what I felt I should say in front of his friends. So I helped her out of the car and told her I was very sorry. She's a sweet girl.

An incident with Jessie at yesterday's dinner table reinforced my despair about my parenting skills. Why am I so unresilient when it comes to seeing my children's weaknesses? It's a feeling of hopelessness: "They will always have terrible manners" leading to its corollary, "I must be a bad mother." Is it simply awareness of failure, albeit temporary? That's something I'm not very skilled at accepting in myself. I know I can't live vicariously through my children, but I would like them to be decent and well-behaved. And kind. And other things. Perfect, maybe.

July 5   Tuesday

Rosemary, a friend of the children who had come up with us on the train, flew home today. I was surprised to find myself daunted by the thought of driving a two-hundred-mile round trip, and so Lin drove us to the airport. I would have run out of energy before I ran out of miles. We stopped for lunch at MacDonald's. A special treat—there are no fast-food restaurants in Carney. (There are no restaurants in Carney at all.) Jeff has an almost insatiable appetite. *How can I afford to keep him? He has already outgrown the jeans I bought him just weeks before leaving Austin.*

Lots of mail today, including an insurance check. I knew it was coming, but somehow seeing it repulsed me: blood money. Given the situation, I'm grateful for the money, but— no need to state the obvious.

July 6   Wednesday

I woke this morning dreaming that Jim had suddenly reappeared: it had all been a terrible mistake. I was overjoyed, filled with pleasure to see him and be with him again. I moved into the day feeling comforted, emotionally satisfied, content to let it be only a dream.

Priscilla, my cousin's widow, has come with her children to spend a few days with their grandparents. We drove to a nearby town for lunch, on the way listening to a tape of Roy's funeral which had been held in the Carney church the same night as the funeral in Madison for Jim. It was a joint service of sorts, acknowledging the same-day deaths of two young fathers who shared connections of faith and friendship as well as family ties. Two young widows commiserating together, a sharing of hopes and dreams destroyed, and the fears and frustrations of suddenly parenting alone. It was a good time with a special friend.

Grandpa helped the kids build a picket fort in the back yard this afternoon. It's so good to be here with uncles and a grandfather around, attending to some of our needs for maleness. Strong arms lifting them into the back of the pickup, deep voices speaking their names, urging them on; the whiskery-scratch of a cheek against theirs; large hugs that make you bend your head back to breathe. There's a feeling of security in that kind of gentle strength. Security, stability, safety, giving them the message that life is okay. Finding appropriate and adequate ways to fulfill our needs for maleness when we return to Austin will be more difficult.

And for me? I don't want to detract from my present enjoyment of life by preoccupation with an active dating life, or with remarriage. I don't have much history of singleness and independence; I started dating Jim when I was still in high school, and we married before I graduated from college. I need to learn to live today, without the presence or active interest of a man. *Lord, make me content with today. And not just content, but really living.*

July 9 *Saturday*

We all spent the day out at Sandpiper Lake, my father's dream bulldozed out of a cedar swamp. It's now a lovely little lake. A strip of sand beach leads to the water, deceptively sun-warmed on top but spring-fed cold beneath the surface. A hundred yards across the water is Lin's picturesque cabin, a century-old structure which she moved log by log from its original site a few miles away. This is home to her even though she plans to spend next year working in Austin and living with us—a generous gift of her time and love.

My youngest sister, Barb, has invited her Spinning and Weaving Group to have their monthly meeting out here today. She is demonstrating the art of weaving ash baskets, a technique she learned from an Indian woman on a nearby reservation. The kids are playing happily in the lake: canoe, rowboat, raft, inner tubes. Endless fun.

It is an idyllic day, perfect weather. Dulcimer and a penny-whistle combine with sounds of children at play, and beneath it all the steady pounding of a mallet against an ash log. The log had been put in the lake a year ago to soak. The mallet raises the grain and allows the more patient among us to remove long strips for basket weaving. Some remarkably good first attempts are being produced, and I marvel at their perseverance.

July 10   Sunday

To church this morning, back to Grandma's for the usual Sunday feast of mashed potatoes and roast beef, then off to Sandpiper Lake for the afternoon. Several uncles and a grandfather helped the children build a new raft, a bigger and better model than the one they'd had before. Fishing, catching frogs, rowing the boat—another great day in the sun. Again I'm grateful for these men in my children's lives.

I went over to spend the evening with Bill and Cindi. My brother marrying Jim's sister created an intriguing doublebond, and I'm grateful for the additional ties to his family now that Jim is gone.

We talked of many things. They recounted to me their feelings at hearing the news of Jim's death: pain for the children and me, but also awareness of Cindi's loss of a brother. We looked together at the pictures of the wrecked cars; by now they held little emotion for me.

But later, as I went to bed, I felt swept away by the "poor me's"—a strong sense of loss and longing as I looked at Jim's picture. I could smell his cologne, and the occasional lingering fragrance of pipe tobacco after a late-evening walk; I remembered the softness of his freshly shaven morning face and the stubbly scratch of his cheek at day's end; I felt the warmth of his lamb-soft sweater, the tweedy texture of his sport coat. And I ached to be held again.

July 12 Tuesday

Ethan slept over at a cousin's house tonight, a relief for me from his bedtime routine. I know it's important, but it's hard to be enthusiastic night after night. Jim traveled a lot, but when he was home he usually took over the bedtime story routines. *Sometimes, after you'd been upstairs an especially long time, I'd follow you to Ethan's room to find you snuggled beside him, book in hand, both asleep.*

Austin friends called today. I was surprised to find myself overcome with tears. I sometimes fear that returning to the "real world" of Austin may be very painful.

July 14 Thursday

A lovely day "on the sea," as Ethan would say it. My father and a friend took several of us in their boats to some charming resort villages across the bay on Lake Michigan. A faulty compass turned a forty-minute trip into an hour and a half. But not to worry—the other skipper had grown up out there and knew the lake like his back yard.

The water in the sunlight looked like acres of scattered diamonds. As we approached the far shore we began to see fishing villages, right out of a picture book. A delightful day of browsing in shops and museums, buying yummies in a Swedish bakery, eyeing marinas of expensive sailboats.

Wouldn't it be fun to marry someone who could keep me in a manner to which I am not now, but could easily become, accustomed?

That pleasant, end-of-the-day weariness that comes of too much sun and fresh air; I go to bed aware that life is full of things to be enjoyed. My occasional fears that I might never again feel happiness are unfounded.

July 16   Saturday

A dream about Mr. B: meeting him, shaking his hand, delivering a "sermon" about his second chance. Is this related to my concern about not having heard yet about the court date? I told Bill I really wanted to be there. He doesn't agree that I should go, but if I insist he says he will take me.

July 17   Sunday   Mackinac Island, Michigan

Lin and I took the ferry to Mackinac Island today; a lovely place, a magical sort of place. *Jessica, this is your sought-for Never Never Land, where change is minimal.*

I cried a few tears on the boat ride over; nothing specific, just a flood of sadness that Jim isn't here to share it. So many memories. The dozens of crossings we made during those two summers we lived here, hauling books, groceries, supplies. Knowing the boxes would be handled a number of times, we chose the sturdiest we could find: liquor boxes. *Remember the comment of the dray driver who helped us move in? "Must be some kinda party you're having."* Afternoons in the park, reading and watching Jim sketch. Riding around town on the tandem bicycle loaned to us by a student. (Days only— he needed it for his social life in the evenings.) Watching the yacht races from our friends' front porch atop the hill, seeing the bright spinnakers drop as the boats crossed the finish line. Wandering around admiring the profusion of boats, and teasing about asking God to call us to be "missionaries to the very wealthy."

Smells: fudge, boat exhaust, horses, fudge, waterfront, fudge. Sights: bicycle porters balancing dozens of bags on the handlebars, horse-drawn carriages, boatloads of "fudgies," the old lighthouse, sails spread to dry in the park below us. Sounds: lines clinking against masts, cannons and fife and drums at the Fort next door, boat horns signaling departure, horses' clopping hooves, and on overcast days the deep warning bellow of the foghorn. There is bittersweetness in coming back to these places of so many memories.

July 19   Tuesday

How many hours did Jim and I spend sitting on this porch, relaxing, chatting, "glassing the harbor," enjoying the view and time with our friends? How good of the Armours to provide us with an "escape" from students, since it was always open house at our apartment. I wonder where the Armours went to escape from us? Before trudging up the hill for a visit, we usually stopped at the grocery for a loaf of bread, a gallon of milk and a bag of potato chips. Though we were newly married, even we could figure out that it took a lot of food to feed four kids (and two rather frequent guests).

This afternoon I slipped out to walk and remember: through Anne's Woods, lush with creeping myrtle and the smell of pine needles; past the Begonia Lady's house; on up the East Bluff Road past all those old summer houses. I stopped in front of our little apartment on Main Street, and tears came as I noticed the bush in the neighbor's yard from which Jim had picked my birthday rose.

Some tears, but mostly a feeling of "ancient history." It was a wonderful time for us, an enchanted place, and I'm very grateful. I recall saying more than once during those summers, "Someday I will hardly believe we actually lived on this island."

I have been assigned Sue's bed, also known as "the cats' bed." Having been warned that locking them out of her room only produces all-night howling, I allowed them to sleep on my legs, though this meant herding them regularly to the foot of the bed, raspy-tongued baths in the night, and at least one of them snoring. Of course they prowled the house and came leaping back up periodically. And these are not your ordinary ball-of-fluff-variety cats—these are heavyweight champs.

We stayed on an extra day to watch the Chicago-Mackinac Yacht Races. Lots of noise and merrymaking last night; most of the boats arrived after midnight. At 3:30 this morning we all went out on the balcony to watch the fireworks which had awakened us. The boats looked eerie in the night, gliding through the water, eclipsing the old lighthouse as they slipped across the spot-lit finish line.

July 20   Wednesday   *Cedar Campus, Michigan*

My pilgrimage continues. It is painful, tearful grief-work to return to those places which hold specific, fond memories of times in my life with Jim. But it brings deep comfort and a sense of release at the same time. The past matters to me, but I will not let it hold me. Recalling the details both momentous and insignificant, the pleasures and the frustrations of making a life together, I find I am awed by the beauty of the fabric woven in our nineteen years of growing in loving. I see the stains and flaws as well, evidence of our lack of judgment, our immaturity or just plain sin. Acknowledged, expressed, forgiven, even those things were somehow used by God to add strength and character. I struggle to come to terms with the loss of that love; it was my life. I am lovingly aided in this process by faithful friends.

Cedar Campus, which is InterVarsity's student training center in northern Michigan, is an important stop on my journey. It was here, twenty years ago, that I met Jim—he an entering freshman at the University of Wisconsin and I a high school senior. For the next ten years we spent a part of every summer here: on work crew, as student campers, as

InterVarsity staff. Walking and talking in the soft rainy night, canoeing, hiking, teaching and singing, laughing and praying. It was here, as a brand-new wife (and feeling very insecure because I was also still a student) that I noted in my journal: "Explore *steadfastness* in the Scriptures; try to understand and apply it to my life." Around me I observed models of mature Christian women, and I was deeply attracted to their stability, their ever-growing knowledge of God's Word, and their determination to live it out in the dailiness of their lives.

So many wonderful friends here; I feel loved, affirmed, encouraged. But the conversations all focus on me, my experience, my children, my memories, my future. I'm not uncomfortable with that, but perhaps I ought to be; it feels very self-centered. Is everyone else really as interested in talking about it as I am? Or are they just humoring me? Are we all struggling to feel a little more in control of this experience by wrapping words around it? Is it a necessary part of their grieving for a friend gone on?

I still marvel, when telling "my story," at God's graciousness. I feel such gratitude and joy at the memories, a sense of being fortunate. Again those questions: Am I really facing it? Could I be denying the horror of it all, performing, spurred on by the awareness of an audience? In stepping out of it to look, I am struck by the tragedy of it. As observer I would be saying, "Look at her spiritual maturity in accepting all this," but as participant I say instead, "The grace of God is a gift." How blessed I feel at the lavishness of his gift.

Pat has come to spend a few days. Friends over many years, we speak of our memories of Jim, and we laugh and cry together. "He was the only truly charming man I've ever met whom I really trusted." And of his foibles: the frustrations of living and working with a man who had no inner clock; his eccentricities, both delightful and frustrating. *How can I keep an accurate picture in my mind? and with the children? How do we remember without enshrining him?*

July 21   Thursday

Spent a pleasant morning with Lynne, a young mother of two little girls. Her husband died of cancer just six months ago. Soul mates. We talked of single parenting, dating and remarriage, coping with imposed celibacy, funerals and other rituals. In talking about the traditions of widowhood, I discovered that my wedding ring does fit on my right hand. *What proportion of that ten pounds came off my finger?* Both of us being novices at this, we're not sure, but we think that symbolic switch from left to right ring finger indicates "widow." I had felt ready to remove my ring from my left hand but was reluctant because it never fit any other finger, and I wasn't ready to put it away. Jim had made it for me out of gold from old family jewelry. He had incorporated his own fingerprints into the ring's design.

We discussed the questions without answers, like "Which is harder: sudden, unanticipated, unexpected loss or long, drawn-out, inevitable loss?" Pain is pain—individual, unique, unmeasurable. And of course we asked the inevitable "Why?"

We agreed our lives feel like a jigsaw puzzle—the pieces all scattered about, only a few in place (and those seem to be face down). *Who can help us? Who has the box with the picture on the lid?*

July 22   Friday

This morning I "did the ashes," scattering them at the base of the bell where I first met Jim. Why has it been important for me to have a man with me whenever I do this? And the bit of ritualizing, wearing Jim's wedding band on a chain around my neck. It wasn't the same deep pain of those first times in Colorado; this time the anticipation was almost worse than the event. I felt it building all during breakfast and on the boat ride across the bay. *What is "it"? tension? anxiety? It feels most like fear.* Afterward we stood together, Keith and Rusty and I hugging and crying. Keith prayed. "He was like a son to us."

Mark, their son, took me sailing. It was a sunlit, gusty day. I enjoyed it but felt embarrassed at my usual tinge of apprehension. It would have been more than a tinge if Mark wasn't such a good sailor. We recalled his days of living with us while he was a student and an InterVarsity chapter leader at Michigan State University; he spoke of his strong and rare friendship with Jim. I delivered my now-standard lecture to friends who are also husbands: "Wills, Insurance, and the Need to Affirm Your Wife." (Subtitle: "After You've Done the

Paperwork, Silky Lingerie and Romantic Evenings Are Great Additions to Any Marriage.")

Having accompanied Jim on more than one canoe trip, a place where Ziploc bags are invaluable, Mark approved our choice of packaging for Jim's "final journey": "I can't think of anything more appropriate."

Tidbits from one of the afternoon's conversations: Just as one experience of sin doesn't constitute a habit, so too with righteousness. We need the continuing discipline of obedience in choosing and living rightly. Is this perhaps why God doesn't immediately remove difficulties as we pray for relief? He knows we need repeated practice—"Here it is again, Lord"—to build those foundations of obedience.

My room has had spectacular moon-on-the-bay views all this week. Kneeling by the window tonight I could tell by the moon that it would soon be three months. I looked at my watch: 11:30. *It was just about this time, on the Thursday-of-the-waning-moon, that Jim had died.* A vague hurt, but not the piercing pain of previous months' "anniversaries." *I guess this is called progress.*

My tears come most often in response to feeling genuinely loved by others, in their communication of concern and caring, and less commonly in response to specific memories. I feel a deep sense of gratitude for the memories, not a resentful "Why couldn't it have gone on forever?"

It will be hard to leave this place tomorrow; I have felt healing here.

VII

Happy Birthday to me. . . ." Jessie was crushed when she discovered midday that it was my birthday and no one had told her. Dad isn't here to remind them of special days. A few hours later she emerged from Aunt Teri's kitchen, cake in hand, triumphant smile on her face. Rituals matter to this daughter. Bless you both.

In church this morning Ethan was unusually clingy, and so I held him on my lap instead of insisting that he go to Junior Church. It appears one can hardly give a child too much hugging. This clinginess, and the occasional lapses into baby talk which I have seen, are these just his ways of coping with the hurt? *Lord, how can I understand? But even when I don't, help me to do the right things, at least most of the time.*

For a while this morning I worked on an analogy of grief as a float trip: some terrifying rapids, a surprising number of sunny days on quiet pools—but with the vague feeling of a dark presence lurking just beneath the surface.

July 26   Tuesday

Dream fragments: As I walk down the street, I find I am clad only in my pink Oxford-cloth shirt. (At least it has long sleeves!) In another dream I'm driving a huge unwieldy car, and I discover it has no brakes. *Am I feeling unprepared? out of control?*

My early morning walk took me up the hill to Barb's garden; a raspberry patch is a good "musing" place (and the jam will be wonderful this winter). A quiet time, undemanding work. The ripe berries plop softly into the pail; I hear the birds singing and the wind stirring the hayfield across the road. Some of my soul's ache eases away in the early morning freshness.

July 29   Friday

A letter from friends in Texas; as I opened it a newspaper clipping fluttered to the floor. Mr. B is dead! *How could he be out of prison? Had he been drinking when he tried to race that train through the crossing? And the passenger who was also killed—whose mother or daughter or friend was she?* The strength of my reaction surprised even me. I stormed out the front door. *Okay, Lord, now I'm mad! Somehow I thought we had a deal here—Jim's life for Mr. B's second chance.* Bad theology I'm sure, but somehow it had made the loss more bearable.

My children have been praying for him; how do I explain this to them? The culmination of a lifetime of bad choices. At least three people have been killed, with many lives dramatically altered; who knows how many other lives have been taken or damaged by this man's destructive living? But I find no satisfaction in this "justice"—only more sadness and a feeling of incompleteness.

August 1   Monday   *Milwaukee, Wisconsin*

More firsts for me: I drove a borrowed car through an unfamiliar city. *I think all these experiences may be adding up to a more adequate view of myself.* Jim had always done the driving, especially in unfamiliar territory, and I had only rarely and reluctantly borrowed anyone else's car, particularly if it was large and/or had an automatic transmission. We always preferred our manual transmission; *some of us don't adapt very easily. But that was in the days when I had the luxury of refusing.*

A letter had arrived for Jeff while he was away at camp. It was from one of Jim's friends and coworkers, and so I should have anticipated that Jeff might want to read it in privacy. But

I was curious, and so I handed it to him immediately, in the press of cousins and friends. After reading a paragraph he left the room. How insensitive of me not to wait for a more private time. I felt very bad and offered my futile apologies.

Dear Jeff,

The morning I found out that your dad died I knelt by my bed and cried for over two hours. I miss him a lot, and I know that you do too. It must be so hard to be without your dad. I pray for you every day.

Jeff, you already know this, but your dad was very, very special. He was special to me because he encouraged me when I was a student. We studied the Bible together, and we went out on campus to talk to students about Jesus. Your dad taught me a lot about how to be a follower of Jesus, but he also taught me a lot about how to be a father. And since I'm getting married this fall, I'm looking forward to having kids like you, and loving them the way your dad loved you. You know one of the best things that I liked about your dad? He liked to touch people and be close to them. It used to make me feel so good when he would sit next to me because he would sit close—and I knew he liked me.

Your dad was very special, Jeff. Be glad that you were old enough to know him—because in some ways—you will be like him.

Love, Phil

Soon after our arrival at John and Linda's house I found Jessie in tears. "Uncle John reminds me so much of Daddy, and it makes me feel so sad. . . ." She's quite right. Many people who had never met John had to look twice during the funeral. Even I, stepping out my front door to greet them on their arrival from the airport the day after Jim died, was startled as I first saw John half-hidden behind a tree. A heart-leap that shouted "Jim!" and then the instant, crushing reality. *No. He's gone. And he's never coming back.*

We accompanied our Milwaukee cousins to church this evening. I struggled against the tears during the commissioning of a couple for ministry, remembering a similar service for us in Madison just sixteen years ago. And I recognized a tinge of anger as I asked God why he took Jim when it seemed we had so much to offer him: gifts in ministry developed over the years, an unusually healthy marriage, a stable and happy family. *What can you possibly have in mind that could be better than what we had?* More than a bit impertinent, and a definite minus on the humility scale, but I'm learning that feelings don't cease to exist because I deny them, and surely God knows of them anyway. Acknowledging my anger and speaking the words don't jeopardize my relationship with the Father. I have a big God, and I know he can take it. Shaping the thoughts into words also provides me the opportunity for repentance and forgiveness when needed.

August 2   Tuesday   *Oxford, Wisconsin*

Another milestone passed: today we buried the container holding Jim's ashes in a country cemetery in the small town where Jim had spent so many summers of his growing-up years. The lush green of Wisconsin summer, the muggy heat of an August afternoon, the strong scent of pine needles as we crushed our way across their thick carpet, the whistle of a freight train in the distance. We gathered in the shade: parents, widow, orphaned children, assorted family and friends.

Jessie had come with great reluctance, and we had discussed Corrie ten Boom's illustration of "You don't need your ticket until you get on the train," making the point that God's grace comes to us at the point of our need and not in anticipation of it. As the freight train roared by just fifty yards away, she squeezed my hand and looked up, tears brimming, "Mom, here comes my train."

Scripture. Prayers. Words of comfort. As John gently placed the sealed plastic container into the hole which he and his father had dug that morning, Ethan whispered, "Mommy, I wish we could see Daddy's ashes." The children and I dropped in our wildflowers and then scooped handfuls of sand onto the box. I had anticipated that we would leave at that point, but the children wanted to stay. Under John's direction and with their cousins' help, they finished shoveling and tamping the sand, replacing the square of sod and watering it from a nearby faucet. It turned out to be a family experience. Not easy, but somehow an important part of the healing process.

Interestingly, each child added his or her own bit of significance to the event: Jessica dropped in her "pet rock"; Jeff asked to keep the tamping stick; Ethan found some red sandstone and asked if he could keep it as his "gravestone."

Scripture assures us of Jim's presence with the Lord, but it's so very difficult to relate to, or even to imagine. Somehow it brings exquisite joy—and floods of tears. If only we could have it both ways. He has arrived; Momma and children are still on the journey.

August 3   Wednesday   *Madison, Wisconsin*

T he children went back to Carney with my parents. I will spend a day or two in Madison at Jim's parents' home, visiting friends, taking myself back to some of those places that were important in my life with Jim, continuing that grieving/releasing process.

Breakfast, lunch, dinner with various friends, and time in between at InterVarsity Headquarters greeting still others. Warm hugs, tears, words of encouragement or shared memories—an important time for me. A friend recalled how word of Jim's death had come that Friday morning to the InterVarsity Board and Management Meetings being held in Chicago. These were people who had known and loved Jim and had worked with him over the years. They shared their shock and disbelief, their deep sorrow, tears, and prayers. *Imagine how thoroughly we've been prayed for over these months!*

I walked back to Jim's parents' home on the streets so familiar to Jim during his years at the University of Wisconsin. I walked past the dormitory where we had lived during

InterVarsity's three week Staff Candidate School. That exciting but somewhat stressful time followed our "honeymoon": apartment hunting in East Lansing. Reservations for a stay on Isle Royale never materialized, not getting beyond the Good Idea stage, overcome by Jim's preference for the spontaneous, the unplanned, his Do-It-Tomorrow bent. That time I should have insisted. *Okay, Lord. When (if?) I marry again, how about a first-class honeymoon?*

From an insightful friend, in conversation over lunch: Sometimes when we ask God our Why questions, instead of giving us answers he gives us himself, the Comforter. From Luke 11:13 Even as fathers give good gifts to their children, so our Father gives the best gift, the Holy Spirit, the Comforter, to us as we ask. It reminded me of conversations with Jessie about why I wouldn't allow her to sleep over at a friend's house. "I can give you my reasons, but you won't like them or understand them, and you'd only argue with me. So let's just accept that this is the way it's going to be, and I'm sorry you feel sad." *Is it a little like that, Lord? Only without the impatient tone of voice . . . ?*

And from the same conversation: Often when we ask God for guidance, what we really want is a Guide. My friend told me of a conversation he had with his young son shortly after they moved into their new house. "You can find your way to your new bedroom in the dark by simply turning on the lights in each room as you go." There was an uncertain pause, then, "But Daddy, won't you please go with me?"

"Do not be terrified; do not be discouraged, for the LORD your God will be with you wherever you go" (Joshua 1:9).

August 4   Thursday   *Carney, Michigan*

From a friend: "Grief is multifaceted." How many ways are there for us to feel pain? This afternoon I felt a new kind of sadness, a sense that no one could ever fully appreciate my loss, no one can ever know the wonder of what we had together. *Is this loneliness?* It lasted the better part of an hour. I played at the piano, hung some laundry out on the line, weeping all the while. A new aspect of pain, and I felt willing to indulge it. But I am a bit fearful of making our love and life together, in retrospect, the "impossible dream." It was very good, but not perfect.

Tonight after showers and shampoos, Ethan asked me if we were staying for the winter. When I replied no, he threw himself across the bed in mock despair and said, "Oh, Mom, you're 'espicable!" We all burst into laughter, and he explained that he had picked it up from Daffy Duck. He went on to relate with great glee how Daffy insists to Bugs Bunny that it's rabbit-hunting season, and Bugs insists that it's duck season. *What joy the children bring. I didn't know it could coexist with pain.*

August 7   Sunday

Everyone went out to Sandpiper Lake for the afternoon except Grandpa Johnson and me. At ninety-one he is delightfully alert and healthy; he comes out from California at least once a year to visit. Our several games of rummy (all of which I lost) were interspersed with conversation. He isn't going to remarry because "she'd probably just get sick and then I'd have to take care of her." But he thinks I should. So do I.

As I walked past the kitchen bulletin board I glanced, as usual, at our family picture. I was surprised by the sudden intense pain, the almost doubling-over kind from those first days of grief. Somehow there aren't enough words (in my vocabulary at least) to describe the great varieties of pain. Today it was the stomach-turning kind, producing that urge to bolt, to run or somehow try to squirm away from the source of pain. Impossible—like trying to crawl out from under the labor contractions of childbirth. Agonizing, but necessary I guess, and (sometimes to my disappointment) survivable. Just there, and unavoidable, at least for this moment. Do I need to learn to work with it, sort of "riding" it rather than fighting it, as they taught us in childbirth classes? Sometimes the Evil behind death peers through, and it seems such a horror. It makes me wish I were a screamer. Instead the silent tears slip down my cheeks. Tonight the pain and sadness are specific and profound, not just the vague weeping of fatigue.

On the way into Ethan's room at bedtime I stopped to look at some favorite pictures of Jim. I saw him again, briefly, alive in my mind; I longed to kiss him, and to be kissed. Quiet tears came from a deep pit of sadness.

I walked into Ethan's room and sat on the edge of his bed. He saw my tears and came to me, taking my hands. I slipped to the floor and knelt in front of him. Without speaking a word he put his arms around me, his small hands patted me gently, and he held me while my tears coursed down his little bare back.

How can I describe it? The ache, the pain feel so beyond touching, so out of reach. And it's not like a physical pain, but it's a hurting, a deep hurting. I guess there is comfort in the fact that it can't continue for long periods at that pitch, that the times come and go, and for the most part it will be getting better. *Or will it? Is that certain?* Sometimes it feels like it's worse—perhaps it's just that each time it seems fresh, new, so intense. The only way I can think of to cope with it is to experience the moment, and then go on with living, a rather relaxed affair here this summer: a game of rummy, a bedtime story, a batch of raspberry jam, another load of laundry. The feeling that "life goes on" is a comfort to me.

August 8   Monday

A small family contingent went out to Devil's Creek Pond after supper. This was one of Jim's favorite duck-hunting places, and I had reserved a final packet of ashes to be scattered here. We arrived just before sunset. Jeff rowed the four of us out onto the pond in a beautifully handcrafted wood-and-canvas duck boat that Jim had inherited from his grandfather. The children initially were somewhat reluctant about this idea, but now participated willingly. Perhaps some of the pain was diffused in our preoccupation with the process, as in passing the plastic bag, reminding Ethan not to stand up in the boat, and trying to help him not to spill the ashes all over himself. Both futile efforts. I was surprised to see how concerned Jeff seemed to be about that last issue.

When I asked Jeff earlier why he didn't want to come, he said, "I guess I just don't want to see Daddy go away, if you know what I mean." I'm not sure I really understand, but I'm glad he tried to tell me.

As I read back in my journals I find myself almost relieved to see the variety of feelings. One big component of the pain is fear—a fear that this experience of pain may not be momentary but might settle down on me as a permanent condition, an incurable disease, an overwhelming and unmoving cloud cover. *This time it's got me and it may never let me go.* I need to keep reminding myself, in the midst of the pain, that I can acknowledge it and give in to it because it isn't a life sentence. "Weeping may tarry for the night, but joy comes in the morning."

August 10   Wednesday

Listening to a favorite song this evening brought on a profusion of tears. Again that exquisite sense of loss, and a feeling of having no one to share it with; that one special friend who knew my heart so intimately is no longer here. A strange, almost circular frustration: It's the pain of my loss of Jim in all its different facets which I long so to share with him.

But I can't reach him.

Do I dare hope ever to have another relationship of such deep love and sharing, caring, enjoying? We had worked out a rhythm (albeit out of beat on occasion) but blending, complementing, working together. Now I see my "beat" becoming the dominant one, out of necessity, picking up those themes which went undeveloped in myself because Jim had expressed them for us. I have a curiosity about what God may develop in my life (probably only by pushing me) that hasn't been evident before. Is it a little bit like the stars that grow increasingly brighter with the deepening darkness? Always there, but not visible until the dark comes. *I really want to be open to all of it, eager to grow. Well, is just willing okay for a start? What sort of shape will my "oak tree" take? And for my children? Oh, how I want good for them from all of this!*

VIII

I feel very sad tonight, and very tired—I think they're related. Everywhere loom things either unfinished or threatening demise: My dryer is making funny noises (and it's raining outside). Both toilets are flushing strangely and sometimes not at all. My kitchen cupboards still harbor "critters" in spite of our best efforts to spray them out (and as a consequence my entire kitchen is in a perpetual state of chaos, with the unloaded contents of drawers and cabinets stacked and piled everywhere). An afternoon conversation reminds me that I need to make a decision soon about replacing my car. Suddenly I fear poverty. And I long for someone to be here to take care of us and our big old house with all its needs. Not to mention my children: At soccer practice all the dads were there helping out; a neighbor is encouraging Jeff to be in Scouts again this year. Our world seems full of other women's husbands and other kids' dads.

It's obviously been too long a day—or a week. I've been on an emotional "high" since arriving home, a surprise to me because I had expected re-entry to life in Austin would be very difficult. It hasn't been, and I've had a lot more energy than I had anticipated—until tonight.

Stirring up and leaving unfinished messes around the house finally caught up with me: I was thinking it didn't really matter because Jim isn't here to be annoyed by it. *Did I really keep house all these years just for you? No, not just for you. But it certainly isn't because of the encouragement of your children.* The chaos does get to me eventually: I feel disorganized, sloppy, uncaring. My immediate environment definitely affects my self-image, and right now I need all the help I can get to feel good about myself.

One part of me just wants to run away, to escape. Another voice says, "If everyone would just leave for a few days, I could really tear into it." Guess I'll shower and go to bed, knowing it will all be better in the morning.

Because it's Thursday and the moon is just past full, I know it was four months ago that Jim died. A great sadness wells in my throat . . . and overflows my eyes.

August 27   Saturday

Ethan just crawled into my bed (3:30 A.M.), interrupting me mid-dream. Here are the fragments: We were all five together in a tent or small cabin; Jim had joined us for two unexpected days—a special gift to his grieving family. Scenes of playing, romping, roughhousing, hugging. *Lord, I know how much we need that physical kind of loving; help me find appropriate ways to meet those needs for all of us.*

A quote from a book I'm reading: "There's a vast amount of difference between accepting and being resigned. I've never been one for resignation" (Madeleine L'Engle. *A Severed Wasp,* p. 79)

August 29   Monday

The weather is changing: a cool wind is blowing away the oppressive humidity. I went in to tuck a sheet around Ethan, and it reminded me how Jim and I would often visit the sleeping children upon his return from a trip. When they were small and still new, he would reach into the crib (over my protests) and scoop them up, cradling them gently in his strong and loving arms. We would marvel aloud at their cherubic faces, their whole and healthy bodies. And sometimes, when they were a bit older, if we jostled them ever so slightly and whispered "I love you," they might stir and murmur, "I love you too." Golden memories.

September 2   Friday

A friend came for lunch today. As Karen and I talked, it became evident that she is very unhappy with her life and marriage. "I suppose I shouldn't be saying this to you, especially now, but I really want to leave: leave the kids, leave Don, just get out." Is it worse for kids to live in a "broken home" or a house full of dissension and unhappiness? And, in her words, there is no spiritual dimension to her life whatever. How shall I respond? "Don't your vows mean anything?" hardly seems helpful given her disbelief in moral absolutes. There seems no real hope for happiness in a change of circumstances, only relief from what appears to be almost unbearable unpleasantness.

It frustrates me in a new way now to see so many unhappy marriages. I'm sure there are countless women who would readily trade places with me: to be a widow rather than a potential or actual divorcée. *Lord, it puzzles me why a healthy, happy marriage should be destroyed when, for some other, a spouse's death might actually have brought relief. But your ways are not our ways.*

Ethan has gone through his first days of kindergarten; it's okay, but there's no wild enthusiasm.

He seems to be developing a friendship with one particular boy in his class. He couldn't remember his name, but he must be special because, "Mom, I told him that my daddy died." Sharing that must be a gift of sorts, a giving of an important part of himself.

The PTA committees are on the phones in full force, looking for eager helpers. I want to be involved in my children's school as a willing volunteer, but I remind myself of my determination that this year my primary commitment of time and energy must be in two major areas: family and grief-work. Family: picking up the pieces, putting them together as well as I can, looking for ways to bring healing and wholeness into our life together. And grief-work: "relinquishing the bonds," allowing and experiencing the pain, letting go of the past, living fully in the present with a healthy anticipation of the future. They are inextricably tied together, the family part and the grief part. How often have I wished that I could first concentrate on my own work of grieving and then help the children with theirs. No such luxury. It makes for some rather bumpy places, but I guess that's part of the definition of family: doing life together.

Time and energy—again the linking. Never before have I been so conscious of the limitations of these two commodities, nor of the seemingly infinite demands made on them. They, like money, must be carefully spent on choices thoughtfully and deliberately made.

September 4   Sunday

One of the Communion hymns this morning completely
undid me. It was one we had used for Jim's funeral, and it
invariably brings tears. A friend came to hug me and say, "It
will be a long time before I can sing that song without crying."

September 5   Labor Day

A slow, lazy waking this morning. As the nearby church
bells play their daily morning concert, I am reminded that all
week they have played our favorite children's hymn: "I Sing
a Song of the Saints of God." If we did have air conditioning,
I'd be missing this.

Another quote from *A Severed Wasp* by Madeleine L'Engle:
"Grief—it will never leave you entirely. There will be odd
moments when it will wash over you like a wave. But you must
leave it" (p. 240).

Just now I recalled waking from a dream the other day, and
I could see and hear Jim clearly in my mind. It was his laugh:
deep, rich, with no trace of self-consciousness. A delightful
and welcome gift, even if fleeting.

September 8   Thursday

Several days ago at the library I happened across an article about a Texas rancher who raises exotic African game animals. It began, " He wears $100 blue jeans, $200 hats and $400 boots . . . drives a Mercedes 450 SL. . . ." Because of Jeff's keen interest in animals I had thought of investigating the possibility of a visit there sometime, perhaps when my father (who had spent a year in Africa during the war) next came for a visit. Days later as I was telling some friends about it I remembered dreaming that I had shown the article to Jim, saying, "I think I've found the man who can keep us in the manner to which we would like to become accustomed. What do you think?" Maybe that's when I heard him laugh.

September 12   Monday

A part of a dream in the night stays with me this morning: Jim coming to me, a brief but climactic and satisfying lovemaking. . . . I am left with warm, loving feelings, a reassurance that the female/sexual aspect of myself is very much alive and well.

Not long before Jim's death, I said to him, "The one event in life which I could never survive would be losing you." I don't recall his response, other than to comfort me. But because other people have reacted with such amazement when

I relate this exchange, I sometimes wonder if I only imagined it. Someone once asked if I felt guilty about having said that— a sort of "magical thinking" of our childhood: to say it or even to think it can cause it to happen. Is that perhaps why some people are so reluctant to write their wills or arrange for adequate insurance?

Several unusually handsome men walked through my world today. They invariably remind me of Jim: his tall, well-built body; his masculine good looks. Surely a lot of women no- ticed, and enjoyed, his physical attractiveness—as I think we're meant to celebrate beauty in its varied forms.

I'm rereading *A Grief Observed,* and frankly find it a bit depressing. I can't relate to Lewis's feeling that God is absent when he most needs him—"the locked and double-bolted door." "Don't speak to me of the consolation of religion or I'll think you don't understand." I guess I don't understand; my experience has been quite the opposite. And for that I'm very grateful. But I do identify with some of what he says: "Grief still feels like fear . . . like suspense. Or like waiting, just hanging about waiting for something to happen. It gives life a permanently provisional feeling. It doesn't seem worth start- ing anything."

Last week a neighbor inquired about our summer, com- menting that it looked as though it had been restful and healing for me. "When you left you had Hurt written all over your face."

September 20   Tuesday

Bonnie has come to spend a week with us. What a wonderful gift a "best friend" is, even across many miles and through accumulating years. That first evening we talked for hours: about our lives, her life, feelings, people, ideas, issues. With laughter and tears, we recalled the past and speculated about the future. And with regard to the present; Bonnie said, "I'm struck by the normalcy of your life here. Jim's absence is very real, but your and the children's lives seem so normal; I'm really quite relieved."

In one of our conversations this week, we talked about whether or not Jim is aware of the details of our lives. Does he celebrate with us the children's accomplishments? Does he see Ethan's growing confidence on his bicycle after all the hours of running beside him that Jim—and then Jeff—did last winter and spring? Does he watch Jessie taking cookies or flowers to the little lady across the street who is homebound? We agreed that if it could possibly make Jim any happier to see his family, he would know and be aware of our milestones and accomplishments. I don't have a theological defense for that idea, but it brings me comfort. And it reminds me of asking my mother long ago if I could take my toys with me to heaven. "If when you get there you still want them, I am sure you can have them."

Last weekend a family from Dallas visited us, long-time friends and coworkers with Jim. They had mentioned some of the same feelings Bonnie had expressed: reluctance about coming, relief to see how well we're getting on. Is that a common fear among our friends—a hesitancy to approach us or to get involved, a fear that our emotional pain and neediness may be overwhelming—a "what if they need me and I don't know how to help" sort of feeling?

How grateful I am for friends who will reach through that hesitation, those who come to us without thinking that they are somehow responsible to fix everything. They can hear our pain, see our needs, and love and support us without feeling guilty that they can't make everything right. Because they can't. But our mutual understanding of this allows me the freedom to acknowledge the hurt and fatigue and grief without fearing that it will send them away. And each has something special and unique to offer, some gift of love that helps us move on.

September 24   Saturday

At 9:25 I was ready to go meet someone for breakfast when the telephone rang. It was Jessie, who had spent the night at a friend's house. "Mom, I came to the university with Amy for her violin lesson but I just remembered that I'm supposed to be at Shari Lynn's birthday party at 9:30." She wasn't exactly sure where she was, but I managed to find her in spite of the streets barricaded for football-game traffic. We rushed home for a gift from the "emergency box" in my closet, drove to Shari Lynn's and braided her hair as we walked from the car to the front door. On the way home I picked up Jeff from Ben's house so he could watch Ethan until Bonnie and Lin returned from running errands, at which point they would take them all to Jeff's soccer game. I managed to get to breakfast only half an hour late, but the orchestration of comings and goings exhausts me.

It's very tempting to think it would be simpler if Jim were here, but my memories tell me otherwise. With only one car, we often worked at cross-purposes, he needing to run work-related errands (often drifting by the local gun shop or used book store on the way home) at the same time that I wanted to go grocery shopping or needed to take a child to piano lessons or gymnastics. *Lord, keep our memories accurate and honest. Don't let our life with Jim become distorted into the "impossible dream."*

September 25   Sunday

Bill is off hunting this week, so Carolyn proposed a moms-and-kids excursion to a nearby state park this afternoon. We picked up a to-go lunch and then spent a lovely afternoon hiking the trails along the river. When we arrived Jeff reminded me, "This is where Daddy brought me and my friends for my birthday camp out." They didn't see much because it rained, but they did sit up until two o'clock in the morning playing Scrabble in the tent by flashlight.

While cleaning the kitchen tonight, I listened to a favorite

John Denver song. I stood at the sink, weeping. Not self-pity this time; these were "Oh, Jim, I miss you so much" tears. Somehow these tears seem healthy and cleansing, in contrast to the "out of control" feeling that dominates the weeping out of sheer exhaustion. I despise that "over the brink" feeling.

September 27   Tuesday

A letter from friends in Africa today said that they were praying for our family, but especially for Ethan. Various friends have made similar statements about each of us; it's reassuring to know that we're thoroughly "covered." *Lord, I am so grateful for faithful, praying friends.*

A quote from the jacket of Paul Tournier's book *Creative Suffering:* "The lives of sufferers demands permanent courage, a constant expenditure of courage, and since courage belongs in the spiritual economy, the more one spends it, the more one has."

September 29   Thursday

Why is Ethan having such a difficult time these days? I spent an exhausting half-hour trying to coax him out of the car and onto the soccer field for his first practice today. He's not normally fearful of new situations, and he seemed enthusiastic about signing up for soccer. His erratic clinging is a complete mystery to me. It's an obvious cry for help—but for what kind? Speak words! I guess I need to say that to him, but I'm not sure he would know the needs or be able to name them. It reminds me of a Sunday last summer in Carney: As we walked across the street to church, he kept telling me he didn't want to go; I kept reassuring him that it would be fine and that we *were* going. Suddenly, just outside the church door he stopped and looked up at me with tears in his eyes. He reached up his little hand and inexplicably began to tear the pocket off his shirt! I was stunned but I finally recognized his desperation, even if I couldn't understand the reason. The mental image of that torn pocket should always remind me: "Mom, you're not hearing me."

Had lunch with Pete earlier this week. We had to go in the back door of the restaurant because he couldn't negotiate the front steps with his leg brace and crutches. He told me what he remembered of that last day with Jim, who was best friend as well as boss: the drive across the spring-flowered Texas countryside, stopping to watch birds with binoculars and field guide; supper with students, and an evening meeting; heading back to Austin late that night. He recalls little about the crash itself. Will those memories return over time? I told him some of the details of our family life that weekend that he lay near death in the hospital: the telephone call, the friends, the funeral. I wonder if he feels some of the same ambivalence I do? Wanting to help carry the other's pain and sadness but feeling too overwhelmed by personal loss to reach out.

A second lunch date this week with a new acquaintance from my five-week evening class on Financial Planning for Beginners. It was an enjoyable time, but we're both still at the "mutually intimidated" stage; because she is a full-time lawyer and mother of two, and because I choose to be a "career mother." We talked a lot about parenting and I asked her about goals in life. She said, "I don't really know—they always ask that in job interviews. What are yours?" Gulp—somehow I didn't feel prepared to express them without sounding like a spiritual bulldozer. I thought I had rehearsed this when I fantasized other conversations of this nature. But maybe I never got beyond asking the question.

This evening class has been enjoyable and stimulating; it's a whole new world to me. I'm interested in learning, but I'm also certain that I need to find a trustworthy and competent guide through this new terrain of investing and planning for my family's financial future. I always thought I had neither the interest in nor aptitude for the arena of investments—I think, rather, the missing ingredient was money.

After getting Ethan and Jessie settled for the night, I usually climb into bed to read for a few minutes. Jeff has developed a nightly ritual of coming in to sit on my bed to read or study, and we often play a game or two of rummy before he goes off to his own room. It seems the best conversations with children happen when there isn't sustained eye contact, such as when I'm driving or peeling carrots or playing cards. To-night I asked Jeff how he felt he was doing with his grieving. "Pretty well; mostly I'm just caught up in school and stuff. Sometimes when I think of memories of things I did with

Daddy I feel real sad, and other times it makes me happy that we had such good times together." As the game progressed I tried to explain the importance of facing it and naming it when struck by that wave of grief or pain. "That sounds just like what I was reading in my Derini books, Mom: when the enemy knows your name, it gives them power over you." Amen. I'm not sure who won tonight. I think we both did.

October 2   Sunday

I'm continually surprised at how many people, particularly those who haven't seen me all summer, greet me with, "You look so good," or a variation on that theme. Is it because they expect me to look ghastly, dragging my way through life? I didn't look so good when Jim was alive? They never noticed me before? Or is it just the thing to say to a new widow? The first, I think. The second is akin to my college roommate's reply to "You look nice today." She invariably responded, "What was wrong with how I looked yesterday?"

October 6   Thursday

It is 1:00 A.M. It was at this time on a Thursday/Friday just—what?— nearly half a year ago. It seems another world away, forever ago, and yet like yesterday (or tomorrow) that

Jim was with us. But the days have passed swiftly and meaningfully. I have rarely, if ever, felt without purpose or direction, or unwilling to get up and face the day. *Lord, I didn't expect that could be true, and I'm grateful for your lavish grace.* I'm sure that having the children and responding to their needs helps motivate me. But they are growing toward going, and I don't wish to define my whole world and life as only "mother." I like to think that even without them I will still feel a sense of purpose and direction in life; I hope never to lose that.

But today I did feel vaguely sad and depressed, relatively unmotivated, energyless. I didn't have a lot that had to be accomplished, and that's exactly what I did: not a lot.

Dan came by this afternoon—an old college friend, in town on business. Our contact has been sporadic over the years, limited mostly to the annual exchange of family Christmas letters. We went for a walk around the nearby golf course and then joined the kids and Lin for supper at the back-yard picnic table. I tried to describe my feeling of discomfort, not really pain: "It's like a dull sword point in my back—I can't walk or run or squirm away from it. It's just there, nagging, uncomfortable, unpleasant."

Thinking a movie might be a helpful distraction, we discussed the possibilities. A comedy? "No, I'd rather see something sad and cry over someone else's pain for a change." So the three adults went to see *Fanny and Alexander*. It was very good: confusingly, stimulatingly Bergman. During the husband/father dying scene, Dan gently took my hand and after the movie he hugged me. I wept into his shirt with soft, involuntary moans. We went out for dessert and talked of many things: about Jim, about grief; of Dan's reaction when he heard the news, his anger toward the drunk driver, his memories of losing his own dad when he was a teen-ager; of his tears as he aches for the children who need to be held and touched by a man; of my associations of pain and comforting with my newly redecorated living room and its new-wood smell of pine shutters and vanilla candles.

As I got out of the car and turned to go in, I hesitated and then reached for a hug from Dan. I was comforted by his welcoming arms, long and strong; the whiskery maleness of his chin in my hair, against my cheek; his words of encouragement, "Someday you will love again, and he will be a fortunate man." He held me for a long time (I almost giggled as I remembered how my neck would strain from Jim's tall embraces), and I felt loved and understood. But as I turned my head on his chest and heard his heartbeat, I felt a surge of deep longing for Jim. "It feels so good to be hugged." I could hear his smile as he replied, "And by a big person?" "Yes, I knew you knew." It intrigues me that those manly hugs can be so uncomplicated and nonerotic for me—they just feel good. It comes later, alone in my large bed. I feel the emptiness beside me. And I ache, deep in my soul.

October 9   Sunday

We all slept in today, skipping church. I have slept badly for several nights—unusual for me.

Last week a friend greeted me with a warm hug. "You can always hug a widow," he said with a twinkle in his eye and a loving smile toward his wife. That could be a bumper sticker.

In my counseling session with Tom this week we discussed the possibility of there being an almost quantitative amount of pain to be worked through in grieving. The only way to the other side seems to be through it, and my intent is to approach it head on, working on it thoroughly and completely, with hopes that I won't someday have to retrace those steps, but can move on into the future. But won't life always have the threat of new pain, the risk of further hurt—if it's fully lived and includes anyone but myself? Caring for anyone (and even some things) necessarily carries with it the risk of hurt and pain, disappointment or loss. Am I willing to accept those risks, to reach out and embrace life fully? I think so. I am not as afraid of pain as I once was; it has the power to hurt, but it doesn't have to destroy me. I'm not out looking for pain, but I know now that I can survive it.

For this month's book-discussion group we read *My Antonia,* by Willa Cather. During our meeting last week the point was made that it is in loving that we enlarge our capacity to love. It's not a quantity to be used up, or a capacity to be diminished, or even a space which can be filled up by a certain number of people. Rather it belongs in the spiritual economy of "the more you give away, the more you have." Giving love expands our resources of love and our ability to love. It enlarges our capacity to love and be loved.

I am intrigued by a quote from Cather's book: "Some memories are realities, and are better than anything that can ever happen to one again." Interesting, but I think it could produce a somewhat defeatist approach to living. Those comparisons can only be made in retrospect, and think what I might miss in life if I decide that nothing can ever be as good as what I once had.

IX

October 17   Monday

A restless, seemingly sleepless night. And a morning dream: Going somewhere on a bus, I saw Jim conversing with friends out on the street. I swung off the bus and we embraced, not longingly, but joyfully and thoroughly, mutually communicating health, well-being, vitality. The bus turned around and I stepped back on with a sense of "All is well—and all will be well."

October 20   Thursday

Tonight we arranged a popcorn party at the neighbors to

watch a movie on their VCR. I forgot the popcorn. But the movie was good, and it made me realize that every movie I've seen in the last six months has included something about death. Is that a relatively new trend in film-making, or am I just newly sensitized?

I stopped to look at new cars this afternoon. No one paid me much attention, just handed me a brochure and answered some questions when I persisted. *Surely what I've heard isn't true—that they won't take you seriously unless you have a man with you?*

October 21   Friday

My dreams are branching out into black comedy: the funeral home brought over Jim's body, sheet-covered, on a gurney, a bandage over his eyes. They had apparently "made some mistake . . . terribly sorry. . . ." I was quite angry with them. Whose ashes were those I had scattered and buried?

October 23   Sunday

As I knelt to receive the Eucharist this morning, the priest placed his hand gently on my head. With the tip of his thumb he traced the sign of the cross on my forehead. "In the name of the Father, the Son and the Holy Spirit." Ancient symbols, ancient words. Ordinary hands, but an extraordinary God. A moment of blessing.

October 25   Tuesday

J essie's birthday, a tough one for her. How can I help her move past the sadness to know—and feel—she's really loved?

October 28   Friday

A semi-anniversary: it has been exactly six months since Jim was killed.

Only a few days ago I completed my three-page "report" to friends: optimistic, basically cheerful and positive, "the glass is half-full" approach to life. That is an accurate depiction of how I feel most of the time, but not tonight. Depression was an unfamiliar visitor. Real depression—that deadly lethargy, the frightening inertia that hangs like lead weights on one's every move—has been mercifully infrequent and short-lived for me. But each time, and again tonight, that nag of fear raises its head and I ask, "Has it got me this time—never to let me go?" Six months ago, depression was not something I was practiced in handling.

When I try to discover what it is, I'm hard-pressed to describe it. A feeling which words won't fit around, a rather vague, nonspecific heaviness, an inertia. A hurt with no cure. Go to a movie? read a book? call a friend? Nothing appeals to me. Instead I give in to wracking sobs as in those first days. The scenes reconstruct themselves in my imagination: the screaming sirens and night-splitting lights; the urgency of the rescue team and the ambulance and the emergency room with its efficient, scrubbed, antiseptic setting. It's only helpful if you're hurt and getting better, cold and impersonal if you're dying. *Was anyone there to hold your hand as you made the transition from this life to the next? How I wish I could have been there to hold you.* Again the sobs. Why do I cry? Because there isn't anything else.

I want someone to call me, to hold me with words. But I don't know who, or I'd have called the person by now. Besides, I'd be wasting my money on tears.

October 29   Saturday

I look around in hopelessness and despair: I will spend the rest of my life shifting things from one pile to another, never really putting anything away. It rarely seems to go anywhere out of sight—just new piles in new places. I hate myself. I will die of pile-itis.

Charles called to invite me to an Italian meal at his house. I accepted because I needed a reason to shower and get cleaned up. I was miserable company, but at least I didn't stay long.

From a conversation with Ethan: "Mom, when I grow up I want to be a preacher just like my daddy." "And what will you do then?" "Tell people about God."

Jessie brought home a paper she had written for a Halloween assignment: describe the scariest thing you can think of. She wrote about being told her daddy was dead. She described our sitting together on my bed and recounted my announcement almost word for word. I had thought the words wouldn't matter, that my children would only remember the hurt. "But first I want to remind you of two very important things: God loves us very much, and he doesn't allow bad things to happen to us without being there to hold us up." *Thank you, Lord, for those words.*

From my morning Bible reading in 2 Chronicles 34, I read of King Josiah's commands that all the people will worship and follow the Lord, even though they don't really understand what they are doing. Does this apply to my children? When they protest going to church, claiming it doesn't make sense to them, am I right in insisting that we go to worship together, expecting and hoping it will bring them to a clearer view of God? Am I doing the right thing? Might it also apply to me? Does my acting in obedience, even when I'm not sure why and I don't really want to, help to bring me to the place of understanding? The devotional guide closed with a helpful reminder from Proverbs 3:5-6. "Trust in the LORD with all your heart and lean not on your own understanding; in all your ways acknowledge him, and he will make your paths straight."

October 30   Sunday

I'm tucked up in bed early tonight, relieved of my regular bedtime routines by Ted, a friend from church. He's now playing a game with Jeff and Jessie, after having read a bedtime story to Ethan, after having carved jack-o-lanterns with all three of them. He's a wonderful man, taking seriously the biblical admonitions to care for widows and orphans. The kids are very fond of him. As he walked into the kitchen tonight he grabbed up Ethan and threw him over his shoulder—that man-handling is so good for Ethan. *Thank you, Lord, for thoughtful friends.*

November 3   Thursday

We managed to pull off another Halloween—my least favorite holiday. I feel at a decided disadvantage in the creative costuming department, and I simply refuse to buy them. Jessie made a great Peter Pan in green tights and a home-sewn tunic and hat. (Or was it Robin Hood? a Junior Jolly Green Giant?) Ethan did his army thing with Jeff's recycled Scout shirt. And five minutes before they left, Jeff decided to go after all and resurrected last year's safari hunter outfit. They all trekked off for trick-or-treating with the neighbors. I felt so weary that I couldn't even face the prospect of handing out treats at the door. *I wish Lin were here tonight.* I considered simply turning off all the lights, but when Ann called I cried, and she offered to come relieve me of my evening duties. A long soak in the bath and then to bed. *Friends, Lord. Again my thanks.*

November 6 Sunday

I spent an hour at Tim and Kathy's this afternoon; for some time I have wanted to ask Tim for more details, to walk back through that night six months ago. Did anyone see the accident happen? Who called the police? If it was a community volunteer rescue team, how quickly could they have arrived? If Jim wasn't killed instantly, how much longer did he live? Did he ever regain consciousness? The doctor was gentle, sensitive. Yes, there was a house nearby and they heard the crash and called. The emergency crew was there in about ten minutes, but they had difficulty removing Pete, who was trapped in the car. The head injury rendered Jim immediately unconscious, and he died within minutes. *But was anyone there to hold your hand?* A loving friend wrote to me, "I know it must hurt that you couldn't be there, but I'm sure Jim was held in the strong and tender arms of Jesus." *So be it, Lord.*

I went on to the five o'clock service at St. David's Episcopal Church. I find such comfort in that service—because it's somehow an echo of the funeral? The same music, the same liturgy. And tonight as I received the bread, "the body of Christ, the bread of heaven," huge tears welled up from somewhere deep inside. The priest set down the paten and took me in his fatherly arms until I stopped crying. *Lord, your eyes and arms in this world, to see our brokenness, to reach out in love and caring. The body of Christ.*

And the closing prayer: "Send us now into the world in peace, to love and serve you with gladness and singleness of heart. Through Christ our Lord. Amen." Not for nothing have I prayed this prayer these past months, regularly and with all deliberateness, conscious of each word. Peace. Love and service. Gladness and singleness of heart. *For you, and because of you; make this true in my life, Lord.*

November 8   Tuesday

While I was getting dinner tonight, Jeff reached up to get the tortilla warmer from a high shelf; the lid sailed to the floor and shattered. For a moment we were both stunned to tears and speechlessness. How can the breaking of a mere thing have such an effect on us? It had been our last Christmas gift to Jim; the children and I had gone to a local potter's shop to pick it out. I tried to comfort Jeff, telling him it didn't really matter. But we both knew it did, at least for the moment.

I had a routine conference with Ethan's teacher today. Both Jeff and Jessie were in her class, and she suggests that Ethan is quite different from his older siblings: more outgoing, free to be himself. (Translation: Getting his name put on the board for excessive talking doesn't particularly ruffle him.) She told me of a conversation she had overheard between Ethan and his new friend: "My daddy was killed in a car wreck. What happened to your daddy?" "Well, he committed suicide." It seems Ethan and Michael frequently put their mats side by side in a far corner during rest time. All through the year, Ethan's response to "How do you like kindergarten?" has been "It's okay—but I don't like nap time." I had attributed that to the fact that he never was a good napper. But now I find when I ask him if he ever really cried because his daddy is gone, he replies, "Yes, in kindergarten during nap time lots of times I lie on my mat and think about my daddy, and that's when I cry."

Jeff has been invited to go hunting next weekend with Tim and his son, Ben. Eagerness is written all over him.

November 13   Sunday

Yesterday Lin and I finished repainting Jim's office—now to be called the library. It's a comfortable blue, and we've rearranged the furniture, removing one of the desks. Last weekend we painted the living room. I'm tired of the upheaval and the paraphernalia: ladder, drop cloths, brushes and tools, pictures standing on the floor. But I'm pleased with the effect, and surprised at the progress we're making. Jessie, however, doesn't like anything about the changes and insists that we should put everything back the way it was.

After several phone calls I finally located the potter who

made the tortilla warmer. I told her my story and she is eager to try to make a replacement lid—but refuses to let me pay for it. Lord, you've populated my world with lots of good folks, friends and strangers.

November 15   Tuesday

Listening to a tape by John Claypool today prompted thoughts about loving and letting go. All of life is Gift—ours to use, share, enjoy, but never to own. I must learn to hold without grasping, to embrace without clinging, to love without owning.

Perhaps it's easier to release those we love when we've had a healthy relationship without a lot of "If only I had said or done . . ." Is grieving the loss of a good marriage (or parenting or other relationship) somehow "cleaner" than if there had been a predominance of painful memories, with no opportunity for restoration and forgiveness? "Clean grief"? Is it the difference between surgery done with a sterile scalpel and amputation by hacksaw?

November 18   Friday

I seem to be coming down with Jeff's bad cold: a persistent sore throat and dragged-out feeling.

This morning after the kids went off to school I stepped into the shower. Moments later the door opened and I heard a little Ethan-voice: "Mommy? I've lost my new glasses." So he and Lin retraced his route to school. No glasses. As I was drying my hair, the telephone rang: it was the neighbor, telling me they had found our cat in the street, dead.

I dressed and went over with a shovel, garbage sack and a cardboard box. It looked like our cat, but how could I know for sure? I loaded it up and drove home, with tears for the children. *Lord, why do we have to live in this broken world, where stuff gets lost and pets and people we care about die?* I walked back to school, looking again for the glasses.

How can I tell Jessica about her cat? How can I help her do another funeral and burial? I dreaded the moment. Later this afternoon as I tried to nap, I heard Jeff and Lin out in the leaves, picking pecans. "Hey, Mom! The cat's back!" A resurrection? No, just a case of mistaken identity. Relief—spelled LIVE CAT. Now what do I do with this dead one?

An incident just before supper added to my burden of the day: a misunderstanding with a neighbor's child, an undeserved scolding from the mother, and Ethan arrived home deeply hurt. *Why am I so vulnerable about these children? Isn't my own pain enough for me?*

After supper I retreated to my room. The accumulated events of the day weighed heavily on me. *I feel like a broken doll, so hurt, so helpless.* And I feel a tinge of anger, but I find myself reluctant to face it, fearing it might open into a yawning abyss. I'm afraid to deal with it . . . and afraid not to.

November 19   Saturday

Ted came to take Ethan for a morning excursion; out-of-town friends arrived to spend the weekend; someone dropped in to offer us their extra tickets to the football game; an older widow-friend wrote to say, "I've cried more tears for you and the children than for myself in my loss." I added up all the evidence to convince myself that I was loved, but still felt powerless to change the feelings. During a picnic lunch in the back yard, a special friend called. I sat on the sunny floor of my bedroom, and we spent an hour talking, laughing, crying. *Thank you, Lord, for that wonderful gift of friendship, for that phone call which enabled me to appropriate all the other evidence and to genuinely feel loved. It turned my day around.*

November 23   Wednesday

Roger arrives from California tomorrow to spend the holiday weekend with us. Friends from high school years, we've exchanged letters and phone calls in the last few months. A brief visit in Carney last summer was our first contact in a number of years. We share a mutual curiosity to explore the possibilities for the future, and I value the candor with which we are approaching it.

This last week I've pushed extra hard to get my house in order, knowing that he is the first in a month-long succession of holiday visitors. We all love having guests, but I'm afraid I may be paying a price—I haven't quite been able to shake this respiratory bug, although the antibiotics have helped a great deal.

November 28   Monday

Roger arrived as scheduled, just before dinner on Thanksgiving. As usual a contingent of single and far-from-family friends joined us for the holiday meal, as well as several of our international friends. It was a relaxing and enjoyable afternoon.

On Friday my cold turned worse and I was sentenced to bed and antibiotics by Dr. Tim. So much for Roger's visit. He and Lin organized the household activities while I installed myself on the couch with pillows and blankets. By Saturday and Sunday I was sick enough to be flat in bed and completely out of it. Roger and I did finally manage to have a fifteen-minute conversation today just before he left for the airport.

Why does my body do this to me? I know all that stuff about my mind and emotions affecting my health, but this was genuine SICK. And a few weeks ago, on my first official "date" since college years, I had to ask Bill to take me home in the middle of an elegant dinner at a favorite restaurant. I barely made it from the car to the bathroom. But that was stomach flu, not anxiety. I arrived home to find Jeff in the same condition—a nervous stomach is not contagious. But are these physical "breakdowns" somehow related to my emotional state?

December 2   Friday

I agreed to do a telephone survey: Question 1. "Are you married?" "Yes. Uh, wait—I guess I'm not. I'm widowed." My response was so automatic it surprised me. Why doesn't it sink in if I'm dealing with it all day, every day? Guess I should expect it to take a while to change the habits of sixteen years.

Today while rearranging something in my closet, I came upon the cardboard shipping box for the container of Jim's ashes ("cremains"). The label read: "We certify that the contents of this box contain the cremated remains of James Lewis Worden by order of Mary Jane Worden." Pain and tears. Why did I keep that box? My frugal nature must have said, "Fine box; may be useful someday. Remove the label and save for future use." I broke it up and put it in the trash.

Now, with the dramatically enforced change in our lives, I can see significant growth in a variety of areas. Why couldn't I have done more of that growing and changing while Jim was alive? Most of it would have pleased him. But might it have thrown off the delicate balance of roles which seem inevitably to exist in any intimate relationship? Or was our marriage flexible and secure enough to have absorbed the individual growth and change which I, at least, had begun to feel a distinct need for? And now, how can I help my women friends expand their worlds, encouraging them in their personal growth without jeopardizing the dynamic tension of living and loving in their marriages? *Lord, give me wisdom in my friendships, not so that I might sound "spiritual" but in order that I may speak truth.*

X

December 8   Thursday

Ted called today. "I'd like to take your kids shopping for your Christmas gift. Have them ready at ten o'clock on Saturday, with a list of ideas and your price limits. I'll use my credit card and give you the bills later." What a thoughtful friend. Of course they're too young to handle that on their own.

December 12   Monday

Mark and Marian are here for a week—what a gift! I didn't think I had the energy to cope with guests after having been sick for so long, and I nearly called them last week to suggest they postpone their visit. Fortunately, I didn't. They came to help: cooking, shopping, repairing bicycles and leaky faucets. And I've been pampered: bubble baths and back rubs, naps, hugs. But the best part has been their help in bringing on Christmas: baking, decorating, gift shopping. Those were all things which I was dreading in earnest this first year without Jim. How could we possibly celebrate? This holiday, more than most, has rituals and traditions which we've developed over the years as a family. How could we do those without him? If it had been left to me, I think I might never have gotten Christmas out of its boxes this year. *Bless you, friends.*

December 14   Wednesday

A dream from my afternoon nap: Jim was beside me, his head cradled in my arm. Reaching from behind, braille-like, I touched and knew again each part of his face; the sense of familiarity was intense. He pulled my bent finger into his mouth, sucking on my knuckle as a baby would on a pacifier—a rare but remembered gesture. Throughout the dream I had a tug-of-war feeling, pulled back and forth from the familiarity of Jim's presence to the reality of his absence. A wrenching, tearing feeling.

Last night the family and several friends participated with the MADD group in a candlelight march to the Capitol, part of a national effort to begin Drunk Driver Awareness Week. Later we watched ourselves on the ten o'clock news. Ethan was particularly noticeable in his white sweater, perched high on Mark's shoulders. A small fatherless boy, looking poignant and vulnerable. Before we left the Capitol that night I very nearly went to one of the television reporters to say, "If you want a story to accompany these nameless statistics, here it is: Three young children facing their first Christmas without their daddy. He's dead—killed by a man driving drunk— and he's never coming home again. Can anyone tell me why our society is so unwilling to do whatever is necessary to stop this waste of human life?" When I proposed my bold idea to the kids they balked, and so I swallowed my imagined words and we went home. I taste them still.

Mark and Marian left today. At one point Marian, urging me to continue regular naps and early bedtimes, said in her best nurse's voice, "You can choose not to care for yourself, but in effect you're asking God to work a small miracle every day just to keep you on your feet." And one day while out shopping I found something that particularly appealed to me. "Buy it," she said, "as a gift from Jim. He would have wanted you to have it."

From a Christmas card: "The Light that shattered the darkness has put together the broken pieces of our hearts."

December 22   Thursday

T his morning I took Jessie to church for a rehearsal of the Christmas pageant. I was browsing in the bookshop when one of the priests came in to greet me. "I need a hug," he said and enveloped me in his arms. His eyes were misty as he spoke of driving near our house recently and wondering how we were all doing. Another warm hug as he whispered, "May the peace of God be always with you." As he left, I turned away and wept.

Why is it so tear-inducing to be genuinely comforted? Not just a "Hi! How are you? How are the children?" But a reflection of my pain in their faces, knowing they really ache for us and wish there was some way they could make it all right again.

My parents arrived today to spend the holiday with us. And, as always when friends or family come for their first visit since the funeral, there is a predictable looking around, a vague feeling of searching for Jim, as if to convince themselves that he really doesn't live here anymore. I usually try to anticipate it, showing them around or encouraging them to wander, pointing out the changes we've made. And I try to make sure they check out the office, the room where he was most frequently found and which is still most visibly his, the walls hung with antelope, elk and whitetail antlers, the zebra skin on the floor.

This afternoon while napping I felt remarkably good about myself, about our life here. But with Mom and Dad's arrival, for some reason, the reality of the loss struck anew. It's a kind of readjustment, a relearning in each significant relationship how to relate as Mary-Jane-without-Jim, a single and not a couple. For almost twenty years we had been as one, or were working toward that end—that's more than half my lifetime. And many of our friends, like Mark and Marian, have known us only that way. In some cases it's almost like building a new friendship. Obviously it's different with my family, but there's a sense of needing to establish myself in a new role, especially in this setting, as head of this family and not as daughter or daughter-in-law, wanting to be parented and taken care of. More unfamiliar terrain to be traversed.

December 25 Christmas Day, Sunday

We did it! Another "first" without Jim—a major holiday celebration survived, even enjoyed to a certain extent.

Last night we picked up several unattached friends at church and invited them home for dinner. Later we exchanged family gifts as we sat before a cozy fire. A pleasant time, a bit strained and subdued—how could it not be?

As today wore on, the traffic increased: back and forth to the neighbors to compare and examine and try out and demonstrate all the new toys, clothes, puzzles, books.

Tonight I indulge myself in thoughts of Jim. I push myself to recall the warmth of his love, the joy of our intimate times, our physical desire for and gratification of one another, our living and loving as one. A blend of frustration and satisfaction, a warm glow, a dull ache, an emptiness and sense of loss, an awareness of the wonder and privilege of what we had shared together. *Lord, put someone in my life who will love me and whom I can love—not out of emptiness or unfulfilled need, not out of my brokenness. Help me to be ready; to be giving, not primarily needing; to be in a place of relative strength rather than weakness. Not my own strength, but yours in and through me.* I want so to live in the present, fully aware and accepting; processing the past, appreciating life's richness in acknowledging memories; anticipating with great hopefulness the future which God has already prepared for us.

December 29   Thursday

Two silly woodpeckers are trying to drill holes in my slate roof. They awakened Ethan, who has spent the last two hours of early morning in my bed. He still comes in at some point nearly every night, but I usually take him back to his own room. He told me of his bad dream: He was out swimming and found he was being chased by a shark. He swam as hard as he could and made it to shore—to his dad and mom, sister and brother.

January 1   New Year's Day, Sunday

How many years has it been since I've gone out to celebrate this holiday? Guess we always felt the best way to start
out the new year was with a good night's sleep.

Neighbors invited us to a family party at their friend's
house—a pleasant evening with fine people. My kids particularly enjoyed playing with new friends, and the hats and
horns and confetti at midnight were a delightful novelty (although I confess the hugging couples brought momentary hot,
blinding tears). I found myself maddeningly self-conscious,
unreasonably aware that I was the only "uncoupled" adult
there. Why did I feel so cautious, so afraid I might appear too
interested in someone else's husband? How ridiculous. Will
I ever regain a sense of equilibrium, feeling comfortable and
at ease again in normal social exchanges? I feel like I'm a
different person somehow without Jim and that I must learn
new ways of relating to people. Perhaps that will come as I
become less preoccupied with what's going on inside of me
and have more energy to reach out and be interested in other
people.

January 4   Wednesday

Another movie, another funeral. *We of the Never Never,*
another great Australian film. I identified strongly with the

female lead as she is unexpectedly widowed, and I envied her opportunity to say good-by to her dying husband. I wept as she wept, reliving the anguish of those first days. The tears coursed quietly down my face, the heaving sobs barely held in check. I found my breathing very deliberate, almost as though I had to remind myself to exhale and inhale. Again I am longing for love, aching for Jim's passionate embrace. It all seems a distant memory, part of a romantic, almost magical past. Sort of like kings and queens and knights and princesses. Like a great book I read once, or a good movie. . . . I hate to see it take on a mythical quality. I want it to be real.

January 6   Friday

Ruth, a coworker and special friend of Jim's, arrived last night. Today we impulsively made a pilgrimage to Caldwell, the small Texas town where Jim was killed. I had never been there before. We stopped at the hospital and found the nurse who was on duty that night. She patiently answered our questions and told us details she could recall.

I was a bit unnerved by her description of the scene: "I arrived just behind the ambulance. The doctor was working on Pete; your husband's body was draped and off to the side. The other man was obnoxious, out of his mind on drugs and alcohol. Here was one man dead and another critically injured, and all he wanted was more drugs. It was disgusting."

We went to the garage where Pete's car had been towed;

to our surprise it was still there. In spite of having seen the pictures, I was still stunned to see how badly it was smashed. The front bumper was just inches off the ground, the steering wheel twisted and right up against the seat. The passenger side was comparatively untouched, only the engine compartment pushed in where Jim's feet would have been and the roof partially caved in. The oncoming vehicle drove right up on top of them. Again the wonder that Pete could have survived. The car is soon to be towed away to be completely crushed; I intend to urge Pete to come see it.

My most difficult moments were the self-introductions: "My husband was killed in that car wreck last April. . . ." My voice caught, my eyes filled with tears. But I was surprised that I didn't have more "pit of the stomach" feelings about it all. It was mostly just matter-of-fact, reality, history. Is this denial? Or have I just been over it all so many more times than Ruth has?

I felt rushed to get home, knowing I had to get Ethan to a birthday party after school, and so we stopped for a quick sandwich to go. Ruth took one bite and gave up; I felt almost guilty for having an appetite.

On the way out of town we passed the stretch of road where the wreck occurred but didn't take time to stop and locate the exact site by searching for glass and debris. I kept wishing I had planned enough time to do that.

January 7   Saturday

J ust before supper last night I picked up a box from the library shelf, and a piece of paper fluttered onto the floor. It was a listing of several checks Jim had written last year. (I wonder where his checkbook record was *that* week?) I was completely undone by seeing his handwriting so unexpectedly. It seemed that he should be there bending over to pick it up. How many ways are there to feel the loss of a love? Tonight it's "I wish he were here with us," just a subtle shade of difference from the more usual "I miss him so" or "I long to be loved" feelings.

I keep hearing this little voice in my head: "Run away, run away." I'm feeling pressed by a myriad of decisions, paperwork, parenting, people. I'd like to get away, but I am daunted by the prospect of arranging all the details to make that possible. So what should I do? Stay here and play martyr? go, and worry about picking up the pieces later? *Again, Lord, you know the end from the beginning, even in the small stuff of our lives.*

January 8   Sunday

O ne of the hardest things for me as "head" of the family may be in establishing myself and gaining confidence in my new role as Chief Financial Officer. A consultation with the parents and in-laws the other day yielded agreement on one point: We need to replace our car. But then we came to a parting of the ways: New car? used car? imported? American made? Will I be able to decide what I think is best for us and then do it, knowing that it will conflict with someone else's opinion of what is right for us? It's obvious that at some points our basic philosophies about life and money differ widely. I appreciate their counsel and advice, and hope that they can be supportive of me even when they don't agree. And even when I make mistakes.

While saying the Lord's Prayer today, I unexpectedly choked on "Forgive us our sins as we forgive others. . . ." I thought I had done that with Mr. B, but it appears that there may be more work to be done in the forgiveness department. *How could I ever have imagined him as innocent victim? And how does one forgive when there is no evidence of repentance or remorse?* I had imagined myself greeting him in the courtroom, shaking his hand and offering him our forgiveness. But what if he had spat in my face—as they did to Jesus? Could I have forgiven him then?

XI

January 21 *Saturday*   *El Paso, Texas*

Having a wonderful five-day retreat with friends here. Quiet mornings (they're all at school or work), pleasant evenings with the family.

These days away have given me time to think more objectively about each of my three, to see from a different perspective some of the habits and patterns that we've established. A little distance in time and space can be mightily refreshing. I was surprised, however, at my ambivalence about leaving home that morning to come here. I felt good about the arrangements I had made for child care, but at the last minute I felt uneasy, as if somehow I shouldn't be going. Was it fear, for their safety or mine? or a sense that no one else could manage life for them as well as I could? Whatever. They needed a break from me as much as I did from them. And I think it might be wise to schedule these trips on a somewhat regular basis—not just wait for the little "Let's run away" voice. It may be too late by that time.

February 4   Saturday   Austin, Texas

I spent the morning looking at new and used cars. No longer is the luxury of ignorance an option. Liters, horsepower, compression, cylinders, fuel injection. . . . Will I ever understand all that stuff? It feels like such a weighty decision, and it has a certain urgency about it, although I don't quite know why.

And yesterday I went—again—to the financial planner's office. He greeted me with a lengthy account of the chaos of his personal life. "All of which is to say I'm still not ready for you." I was surprised. I tried to decide if I was angry. I thought, *What are my alternatives? Why do I so often feel trapped? Perhaps I should "take charge"—announce my anger, add to his misery and take my business elsewhere. Start over, back at Square One.*

So we talked. I shared my discovery from charting several months of spending that our outgo has exceeded our income by a considerable amount each month. He told me that this was "serious." "You can do that, but not for long. I can tell you just how long." Thanks. Agreeing that we're not really extravagant (in relation to what?) and that I can defend all our spending, doesn't help solve my problem. And so it too is in my lap. My lap is getting too full. . . .

There's so much for me to learn all at once, so many decisions that I alone must make. It feels too heavy for me; I can't cope with it. But what are my alternatives? To collapse in tears? to say "I can't"? to cry for help? I'm convinced there are plenty of people who genuinely care and wish to help. But what can they do except listen, offer advice, absorb my tears and wish they could do something to fix it? Today I'm convinced heaven must be endless days in a warm green meadow with a hammock, favorite books and icy lemonades.

Healing. I guess that's what's happening. But I hate it (and welcome it) that Jim feels so far away, only a distant memory; like a great novel or favorite movie to be occasionally brought out and savored. Did he ever really exist? It was so abruptly, savagely ended; the last pages (or was it most of the book?) ripped from the binding. Sometimes the memory is brilliant and shining and real, but more often it's shriveled and inadequate, rather like dried fruit compared to fresh-picked. Not very appealing, but sometimes better than nothing at all.

I can remember feeling very discouraged when I was a sophomore in college; all the excitement and newness and drama had worn off, and the years to the finish line stretched endlessly on. "When I get to be a junior, at least I can say I'm past the halfway mark, and I can endure. But from here it looks interminable." Is this a shadow of that feeling? No longer the ripping pain of sudden loss, nor the tragic figure of widow with orphans; now just the thudding ache of everyday reality: Life Without Jim. Where are we on that course? Where is the finish line?

"Run with perseverance the race that is set before you." How can I run when I don't know where I'm going? I want it to be Perseverance, Steadfastness, Endurance, but I think it's more like Stumbling, Struggling, Crawling. *Can that count, Lord?*

Last week I discussed with a friend a rather sizeable household purchase I was considering. Her husband called tonight to give me the benefit of his rather extensive research. "But Don, I already bought it." He assured me that I had been had by the salesman and went on to tell me more than I wanted to know or could understand. I struggled to maintain my composure, biting my lip to keep the tears out of my voice. His closing remarks were a bit more encouraging, and he offered to try to get my money back, but he wasn't hopeful. "Consider it a part of the cost of your education."

February 8 Wednesday

Both Jeff and I are down with the cough/congestion/fever flu. Lin has been playing private-duty nurse, cook, maid and mother to us all. And the school nurse just called to tell us to come get Jessie—she has all the same symptoms.

A flashback: "Jim, if I ever lose you, I think I will have two major regrets: that I didn't tell you frequently enough and in enough different ways how very much I love you." "And the second?" "I never loved your dog."

February 10   Friday

Day 6 in bed: I have never been sick this long before. But this is a vicious virus. I hear horror stories about people who try to get up too soon, and a relapse sends them back for several more weeks in bed. For awhile I was too sick to care, but now I find my mind plagued with lists and tasks unfinished. Does this mean I'm getting better? Or is it just a trick to get me up too soon? *Don't rush it; give yourself a little more time. . . .*

I know that we are prime candidates for illness this year—emotional stress directly affects one's physical health. But don't I get points for knowing that? Somehow I felt that knowing it, I could avoid it.

Jessie is much better and on her feet today; Jeff is up a bit more too. But Ethan went to bed with an earache, and Lin's throat is getting progressively worse. Who can go to the store for fruit juices and Kleenex?

Tonight my loneliness is so acute that sleep eludes me. As I heard a car door slam outside, I was swept with a wave of desire for the textures and fragrances that were Jim—a deep wish that it could be he returning from a trip, his presence moving up the stairs to wrap me in his arms, my face cradled in the masculine roughness of his tweedy sport coat and wool sweater. If only he could even come momentarily, to hold me and to say "Oh, how I loved you!"

Again the many facets of grief. Tonight it's not the "poor me's" but a simple, overwhelming feeling of loss. The gaping absence of Jim's love—now, and what I had anticipated for the future. It doesn't affect the past but only the Enormous Present; it's a feeling of being engulfed by, almost eaten alive by, sadness.

1:15 A.M. Ethan came in. I was still awake, crying. "My ear hurts, Mommy." He climbed up on my bed and stretched full length beside me to be stroked, held, comforted. Eventually I took him to his bed via the bathroom, a drink and Tylenol. I sat beside his bed and watched while he fell asleep, this orphan-child on the eve of his sixth birthday. More tears. *You ask too much of me, Lord.* And so I knelt by my bed, weeping and praying without words. In the winter-bare branches of the trees outside my window, I heard a distinct but gentle breeze, and it reminded me again of my friend's words over lunch months ago: "He doesn't promise to give us answers, but he does promise his Comforter, the Holy Spirit, to those who ask." And so I ask, again.

Lord, send the gentle breeze of your Holy Spirit into the recesses of my broken heart, sweeping out the shattered pieces, picking up the shards. Bring to my soul your healing. Move me toward wholeness.

February 11   Saturday

I do feel better today. The trick is to try not to feel—or think or do—too much at all until I'm well. Right? I recognize that after a week of putting my life on hold, it's only natural to feel sad and vulnerable. But I'd still like to do something to change it. Call friends? stay in bed and rest to conserve energy? get dressed and go out for a change of scene? I choose the last and the first.

I can't believe it—I haven't had shoes on my feet for a full week.

February 14   Valentine's Day, Tuesday

Definitely a day for lovers. The rest of us are left on the sidelines. But I do feel loved, even if not as completely as I'd like. Dave and Diane sent a lovely arrangement of flowers, and several long-distance friends have called. I am loved, and I'm grateful.

February 15   Wednesday

Had lunch downtown with a friend. She shared her frustrations about an unfulfilling job and her disappointment that she has not yet had the opportunity for marriage and children. It makes me aware that my life has already held more happiness than many people even hope for.

Years ago when staff wives were annually asked to respond to the question, "Are you reasonably content with your husband's choice to serve with InterVarsity Christian Fellowship, and with your role in that ministry?" one wife on our team replied, "No, I'm unreasonably content." I recall just last year telling Jim—and frequently myself—with a certain amount of awe, that I felt so content with my life. Even acknowledging the inevitable tensions and struggles of two separate people making a life together, I considered myself "unreasonably happy."

While I'm grateful for that, I find it takes a tremendous amount of energy to deal with the feelings and memories of the past. Almost anything can trigger a memory which prompts tears. And I find myself continually having to choose—to beat it into submission with "Not now, I haven't time," or to indulge it, interrupting whatever I'm doing to give it attention. It's like having a double life: living in the present while trying to come to terms with the past. Exhausting. At times I almost wish it could all be wiped out, as though it had never happened; the memories and the pain, both gone. I know I wouldn't really want that. How can I even think it? It's easy—nobody likes to be in pain.

In this afternoon's conversation I think I saw a glimmer of change in my attitude about marrying again. From a desperate sort of hoping to be rescued I sense a shift toward wanting to remarry from a position of strength. I'd like to think that I've achieved a certain degree of control and order in my life so that I could come to a relationship saying, "I can do this myself. I can manage on my own, but I'd much rather share my life with you."

Tonight after dark Ethan and I went outside to take the laundry off the clothesline, and we remarked on the lovely full moon. It prompted memories of my last evening out with Jim: dessert, a stroll and cuddling in the hammock under the full moon. . . . Ethan and I picked up the laundry basket and went in to supper. Later as I bent over the dishwasher I suddenly burst into tears. Lin, with her ever-ready hug, asked what was wrong. "It's just that the moon reminds me of . . ." Ethan's pleading voice abruptly broke in, "Then don't look at the moon, Mommy." Please, anything to keep away the tears.

He gathers the lambs in his arms and carries them close to his heart; he gently leads those that have young. (Is 40:11)

February 16   Thursday

How can it still be so painful?! Pete came by to report on yesterday's trip to Caldwell to see his car. In rummaging under the dashboard on the passenger side, he found a mug he had purchased in the student store, some magazines and—he looked at me hesitantly—one of Jim's shoes. He remembered that I had asked about them some time back. The conversation proceeded, full of questions and speculation about the details of that night. Pete tried to recall all that he could: the bright lights, the urgent voices, the grating and metal-ripping of rescue equipment. But of the minutes after the impact, before the emergency team arrived, he remembers little as he moved in and out of consciousness. "I'm not sure, but I think I remember . . . hearing Jim moan." Emotional overload: I excused myself rather abruptly and escaped to my room. *How can it hurt so much to think of another's pain? Again that deep longing. If only I could have been there to hold you!*

In something I read last week I found this quote from a very old tombstone in the Northeast: "It is a fearful thing to love what death can touch."

XII

February 24   Friday

The other night Jessie had to make a quick visit to Hong-Ying and Li-Hua's apartment for help with her report on China. Jeff and Lin were both out, and so as I tucked Ethan into bed, I explained that we would be gone for only a few minutes. When we returned about ten minutes later, we heard Ethan's quick little feet on the stairs and a frightened sob, "Mom?" He rushed into my arms and let loose his little-boy hiccupping sobs. "I thought Jeff was here, but I looked all over the house and I was all alone." We hugged, and I apologized profusely. "That's okay, Mom; it helps me with the brave." So small and frightened and helpless.

A friend just called from Wisconsin; he would like to come down next week to rebuild our stone retaining wall, felled by the creek in last year's flooding. His wife and kids will come along to spend their spring break enjoying the Texas sunshine, while Al and his associate work on the wall. I am delighted, though genuinely puzzled that a man so recently a stranger would be so generous. We met three months ago when a late evening telephone call interrupted my plans for a hot soak in the bath. "You don't know me, but I bring greetings from your friends in Madison. . . ." We chatted for a bit and learned they had come to Austin rather unexpectedly on business, not realizing that this was a football weekend. "Do you know anywhere in town where we can get a hotel room? We've called everywhere." "Of course. We have plenty of room. Come on over." I didn't know how overpaid we would be for that simple offer.

It reminds me of our experience a few years ago in helping a family from Egypt. Dr. Youssef was doing postgraduate work at the University of Texas, and his wife was in the investigative Bible study I was leading with a group of international women. When Magda was suddenly admitted to the hospital with a diagnosis of breast cancer, we brought their two small children to live with us for several weeks. As we and our friends reached out to help, we found them inexplicably drawing back, eventually insisting that we not do any more. We finally realized that in their culture they would not accept what could not someday be repaid; they felt terribly indebted. We struggled to explain: "In God's family, giving is like a river. It doesn't come back on itself but rather moves on, from here to there, and on and on again. At some time you may be in a position to reach out to help another. And if we are someday in need, God will surely provide others to help us." How prophetic.

March 2   Friday

The counseling sessions have been instructive, encouraging, affirming. "I didn't know Jim, but I'm convinced that he was an exceptional man. Now, next week I want you to come back prepared to tell me what you contributed to that relationship. How did you enhance Jim's life?" And several weeks ago he gave another helpful assignment: "An unusual man, yes, but we both know he wasn't perfect. What were some of those things that made him hard to live with?"

March 7   Wednesday

In desperation last week I called a lawyer friend from church for suggestions about finding a new financial adviser. He recommended a man from our church, and I called that same day. An initial appointment took care of data collecting and information exchange. Goals? I'd like the kids to be able to choose to go to college someday, although we had never anticipated helping them very much financially while we were on a minister's salary. I'd like to replace our car. And our intention in setting up the insurance plan initially was to make it possible for me to continue at home as a full-time mother as long as the children were young.

Within a few days Duane and his associate had drawn up a proposal for investing the insurance money, which would provide us with income to supplement our social security and workers' compensation benefits. They also made suggestions about government bonds for each child, maturing about the time of their high school graduation. And I was given clear instructions on how to keep accurate records of our spending over the next several months, anticipating that our expenses will probably be higher than when Jim was with us. *You didn't eat that much—especially since you were out of town at least a third of the time. And now I have to pay someone to fix the plumbing and change the oil in the car. Then there's a weekly counseling appointment. And until Jeff can help me drive, our cross-country trips to see family will have to be on public transportation. On the other hand, of course, we'll no longer be making those occasional "investments" in fine firearms.*

March 9   Friday

I ordered a new car today. It should be here in several weeks. It's exciting to be learning, but it's more than I ever really wanted to know. I just want it to start when I turn the key and get us safely to our destination. It's a whole new world: fuel injection, engine displacement, suspension, disc braking systems, colors, fabrics. Should I get cruise control?

a luggage rack? *Why do I keep asking myself what Jim would have liked? What do I want?*

Tomorrow I have interviews with several accountants, at Duane's suggestion: "You need someone to help you prepare your tax return, at least this first year. Here are several names; call them, arrange an appointment and then choose the one you feel you can work with most comfortably."

These are all new paths for me, new challenges, new lists, new vocabulary—from baby-sitting co-ops and grocery lists to stocks and bonds and engine specifications.

March 14   Wednesday   *Los Angeles, California*

We decided to make a rather extravagant trip to California at Roger's invitation. Disneyland, Sea World, Universal Studios—the usual tourist stuff. We talked through the details of who would pay for what. All the rules have changed since my dating years. Besides, I don't know of any etiquette book that discusses who pays for a "date" to Disneyland with my three kids.

March 16   Friday

Sick again?? I couldn't believe it. But at least I waited until after we left Roger's. I didn't feel very good at breakfast but ignored it and ate anyway. I spent the entire flight with my face in a bag. Jessie was remarkably grown-up and helpful. Another flu bug? Twenty-four hours later I felt fine.

March 20   Tuesday   Austin, Texas

J essie and I went out for our weekly hamburgers after her choir practice. She was in a playful mood and so I risked a light comment to find out where she is on the subject of other men in my life. "I want you to know I gave up a real, live date with a man so I could take you out tonight." "Really? Who?" She kind of giggled and added, "It sure seems funny to think about my mom going out on dates." And later, "I'm not sure I ever want you to get married again." I guess her tentativeness qualifies as progress.

March 23   Friday

F rom a novel about a widower and his family: "The world turns upside down and when you're used to that, it turns inside out" (Robert Kimmel Smith, *Jane's House*, p. 78).

Had a surprising experience at the dentist today. As he carefully probed and drilled and filled, persistent tears ran across my cheeks and into my ears. I shook my head as he repeatedly apologized, "I'm sorry if it hurts." But it wasn't that at all. When he had finished and all the hardware was out of my mouth, I said, "It's just that my face hasn't been touched so gently in such a very long time."

March 24   *Saturday*

Tomorrow is our annual neighborhood potluck Easter picnic, and I'm having my usual night-before anxiety: "What have you done, inviting forty people for lunch? What if it rains? What if no one has a good time? What if everyone brings dessert?" Or is it really Jim's voice I hear: "Why do we have these mob scenes? Why not just invite two or three couples for a quiet, intimate, sit-down dinner party?" But in the past everyone—even he—seemed to enjoy it. And they all seem eager to come again.

Last year Jim's brother John and his family came on Amtrak to spend part of Easter week with us. In nearly sixteen years of marriage we had each had three children, but our paths had crossed only infrequently, and the cousins were nearly strangers. How wonderful that we had finally gotten an extended time together, with opportunity for a number of satisfying and lengthy conversations. As we talked one evening about friendship, I remember Jim asserting that he indeed had a number of significant male friends. Initially I was inclined to challenge that statement. But as the discussion proceeded, we agreed that while friendships between females are typically characterized by a certain level of verbal intimacy and self-disclosure, male friendships are more often built on common interests and shared activities or experiences. It helped me to realize that his friendships looked different from mine but they were no less significant. Months later, after his death, a surprising number of men said to me in various ways: "I will deeply miss Jim; he was a dear friend to me."

April 5   Thursday

Ethan is in bed, bathed and storied; Jessie is in the tub; the dishwasher is humming; Jeff has moved on to his homework; and Lin is rearranging the papers on her desk. It's a quiet, pleasant night. Part of the pleasantness can be attributed to the fact that my room is clean: the piles have been consolidated against the wall, all the clothes are in the closet; I can finally sit in my chair and look over at a "made" bed. Small pleasures. But I should more often acknowledge how differently I feel when my house is clean, my space in order. I think this must mean I need house-cleaning help—to be justified on mental-health grounds.

My occasional ventures out into the world of dating are exhilarating, confusing, and a little frightening. I feel so vulnerable. I met an interesting man through mutual acquaintances, but I realize that Doug is far more experienced in the world than I—and I don't want to become just one of his experiences.

April 13   Friday

I dragged through this day after a seemingly sleepless night: the neighborhood cats had an altercation around three o'clock, a neighbor came in at four o'clock, and whoever owns that stalled blue car came by at 4:30 and tried in vain for fifteen minutes to start it. He finally gave it up and roared off on his motorcycle. Jeff got up at 5:30 to leave at 6:30 for his Latin Club's trip to Astroworld. And I had a breakfast appointment at nine.

I tried to resign myself to not hearing from Doug, all the while hoping it was him every time the phone rang. Talk about an attack of adolescence; it feels like all the worst parts of being fourteen again.

April 19   Thursday

Tonight, after she went to bed, Jessie called me into her room. With tears in her eyes she said, "I miss Daddy terribly, but I think I'm coming to like the idea of having another daddy sometime." So we talked about the idea of adding, rather than replacing.

April 27   Friday

Mark arrives tonight to spend this weekend with us. I'm so grateful for his sensitivity in anticipating the pain of this first "anniversary," even as he and Marian did at Christmas time. A number of friends have called or written; the florist has delivered a lovely arrangement of cut flowers; and this morning Ann came by with a lovely rose of pale coral. As I went to bed last night I reminded myself that Jim died on a Thursday one year ago, just a few minutes before midnight; as I reached up to turn off the light I noticed that it was 11:30. . . . Awareness, but no great pain lurking there, and it seems pointless to try to deliberately dig it up.

And so we go on. Perhaps the weekend will become increasingly difficult. But on the other hand I wonder if I might escape a "reliving" of that time, having just reviewed it all last week while in Madison with some very special friends. During a long, quiet afternoon over tea, we spoke of the details of Jim's death: the accident, receiving the news, telling the children, the funeral arrangements, scattering the ashes. I saw my pain reflected in their faces (or was it their own?), and I felt loved and comforted.

Yesterday Jeff and I went out for breakfast at our favorite Tex-Mex restaurant; then I dropped him off at school. It's been an occasional event which I think we will develop into a weekly pattern. We talked about ways we might commemorate our family's having more than just survived this first year without Daddy; a hot-air-balloon ride struck us as a graphic way to celebrate the resurrection. Tantalizing, and a little bit frightening. My telephone inquiries revealed a number of limiting factors, not least of which was the fact that the basket holds only three passengers. I confess that my disappointment felt more like relief.

April 28   Saturday

Last evening I met Mark at the airport, and we went out for an evening of quiet conversation over dinner. He was coming to Austin on business and thoughtfully scheduled his trip a few days early to coincide with this weekend. It's nice to have friends in secure marriages whose wives don't feel threatened by their husband's affirmation and encouragement of me.

After Jeff's soccer game today, Pete joined us at one of our favorite restaurants where they serve super-size hamburgers on homemade buns. Later we drove to Mt. Bonnell, the highest point in the city, to walk and look around. Pete did well even with his leg braces and cane. A spectacular view—a coward's substitute for a balloon ride.

April 29   *Sunday*

T im and Kathy had thoughtfully invited us to spend this day with them out at their country property: a picnic on the river bank; the sounds of splashing and playing in the placid, sunlit river; exploring the mysteries and intricacies of a nest of daddy-longleg spiders; a hike up a shallow limestone creek bed.

It was a pleasantly near-normal weekend. I kept looking around for those deep feelings of pain, but there weren't any, at least not readily accessible. I know that in the days and weeks and months—even years—to come they will be there, occasional and unexpected. Whether mild or blinding, the pain will remind us of our loss of Jim, but also of the wonder of what we had shared together.

"What's lost is nothing to what's found; and all the death that ever was, set next to life, would scarcely fill a cup" (Frederick Buechner, *Godric*, p. 96).

Knowing this would be a difficult time for Jim's parents, we arranged to have a friend in Madison deliver a pot of spring-flowering bulbs with this note: "Even as we recall the pain of Jim's death, we remember the resurrection and rejoice."

Jeff, Ethan, Mary Jane and Jessica (November 1988).

Afterword

In the time since that life-shattering telephone call, I have learned many things. I know now the high cost of loving. Had I known it on my wedding day, I hope I would not have chosen differently.

I also learned that I can survive pain, even if at times I have wished it weren't so. I will not be dissolved by floods of tears, like a graham cracker in milk. Grief doesn't have to be a life sentence.

The physical effects of grief were a surprise to me. The early symptoms of pounding heart, shortness of breath and stomach-lurching pain eased with time, but occasionally caught me off-guard even weeks and months later. Now, more than four years afterward, it seems a distant grief. The physical pain blurs into the sad memories of that first year.

Suddenly a single parent, I was fortunate to be able to continue full-time parenting without the added stress of finding employment outside the home. While a daily nap seemed essential to me that first year, I realize it was a luxury that may not be possible for everyone. But adequate sleep, healthy eating and regular exercise need to be high priorities for anyone going through emotional crisis. I maintained an inner commitment to attend to my appearance—my hair, makeup, clothes—even though Jim was no longer there to be appreciative. It affects the way I feel about myself, and I think it gives an important message to the children: We aren't going to abandon living because Daddy is gone.

With the encouragement of friends I was able to give myself permission to take care of myself. Arranging regular times away from home responsibilities served me well, providing a fresh perspective and renewed energy. Another important part of taking care of myself was letting go of some of the "should do's" and "ought to's," especially as a single parent. I will always be grateful to Joe Bayly, an insightful friend who himself suffered many griefs and losses. He pointed out, "Don't try to be both father and mother to your kids. Just be the very best mom you can be."

I learned to cope, to some extent, with infuriatingly old plumbing in our house and mysterious interiors of car engines. At least I now know whom to call. I am no longer intimidated by self-serve gas pumps, and I can light my own furnace. But I still pay someone to change the oil in my car. Sometimes I even read the financial section of the newspaper on my way to the comics page to search for fresh clippings for the refrigerator door.

I'd had practice in some of these areas because of Jim's traveling. But I still felt overwhelmed and sometimes terrified by the avalanche of unknown responsibilities which suddenly became mine. I was a freshman in a graduate-level course. Looking for a hammer one day, I walked into Jim's workshop in the garage. I felt as if I were on another planet.

The support of family and friends was invaluable to us, as they came alongside to help carry the burden of our grief. Our years of building friendships within and outside the church family provided a great resource of comfort and help. I learned to accept offers of help, sometimes even to ask when what I needed wasn't being offered. And as our own wounds healed and we began again to reach out to others in need, we found that much is received in the giving.

I was spared many of those well-intended but painful and unhelpful gestures of sympathy; platitudes and Scripture quoting did not make the hurt go away. Nothing could explain why Jim was gone. The helpful friends expressed their love by doing and listening. And they were careful not to rush us through any part of our grieving.

In the back of my journal I made a list of the Scripture verses people had suggested in cards or letters or conversations, and I began to read them many weeks later . . . when I felt ready to receive the comforting words.

The Art of Grief Work
One conviction continues to grow: Because we all suffer losses

of various kinds, the need for grief-work is common to all. But it is also unique to every person. No one could tell me how to grieve or how long it should take. That it needs to be done is certain; the means of doing the work of grieving is individual.

And grieving *is* work: exhausting and regressive. I found it didn't progress in neat and predictable stages but was frustratingly erratic and repetitive. "Every day in every way, life is getting better" does not apply. As I stepped aside periodically to evaluate, I saw improvement overall: a gradual lessening of the pain and fear, a growing confidence in my ability to handle life's everydayness. But setbacks were sudden and frequent those first months. I would often find terrain which I thought I had traversed and left behind me was maddeningly underfoot again. I tried to learn to evaluate life in bigger chunks. Looking back over a month's progress can be more encouraging than too-frequent scrutiny, just as an hourly or daily weigh-in if you're on a diet can be discouraging and self-defeating.

Six months after Jim's death I wrote in a letter to friends:

I am still occasionally swept by an unexpected wave of pain and hurt, the staggering awareness that Jim is not, and never will be, with us here again. But I'm learning that the best way to get to the other side is to go through it, to face it and to name it, to accept the pain and deal with it as directly as I can. I'm also finding, to my surprise, that there are frequent stretches of days without tears, and any feelings of despair have been only fleeting.

Four years later we see evidence of healing in many small

ways. For the first three years we commemorated the anniversary of Jim's death by going out for dinner at a favorite restaurant. As April neared its end this year, we discussed going but chose not to. It just didn't seem that important to us. Our "family of five" portrait still hangs in the hallway where we pass it many times each day. Occasionally we browse through old photos and retell favorite stories. Sometimes still there are tears. The pain has diminished, but Jim will always be missed.

In looking back over that first year of deliberate grief-work, I began to see patterns in my choices and a new principle about life began to take shape in my mind. The principle is this: beauty can help to bring healing. I found myself consistently choosing, when given options, to surround myself with beauty, whether natural or manmade—rainbows, mountains, wooly lambs, an icy mountain stream, fragrances and flowers, a field of bluebonnets, a mound of honeysuckle, a bowl of fresh-cut lilacs, fresh strawberries on homemade ice cream, a carefully arranged bowl of fruit, an elegant table of fine china, crystal and silver, a mug of hot cider with cinnamon donuts, the crisp clean feel of sun-dried sheets. These places and things were somehow soothing to my soul.

I am convinced that God has built into all of us, in varying degrees, the capacity for and appreciation of beauty, and has even allowed us the privilege of participating in the creation of beautiful things and beautiful places. I think it may be one way God brings healing to our brokenness, and a way that we can contribute toward bringing wholeness to our fallen world—appreciating beauty, noticing it, exclaiming over it.

We need to encourage in others, our children and our friends, a sharper awareness of the innate beauty of God's created world.

The children and I have exercised our interest in hospitality by developing a "Bed and Breakfast" home. B & Bs offer an alternative to the usual hotel/motel accommodations, a more personal, family-style experience for travelers and sojourners. Two of our bedrooms are set aside as guest rooms, and we have enjoyed working together to make our home a beautiful place, a welcoming place with a comfortable, simple beauty, not extravagant or ostentatious. We've delighted in sharing our home with a great variety of guests. This is one way we have felt we could minister healing to our world.

I have a new appreciation for the fact that God has designed us with a marvelous capacity for healing. Imagine if every cut finger, scraped knee or broken bone stayed with us for a lifetime, painful and incapacitating. Instead he is the gentle healer of our wounds, emotional as well as physical.

Last summer I took the children, in spite of their lack of enthusiasm, back to Wisconsin to see Jim's grave. The gravestone, selected in Austin and quarried from Texas marble, had been inscribed to say simply: ALLELUIA, James Lewis Worden, June 28, 1945—April 29, 1983.

Several months ago I found myself back at the family cemetery plot as Jim's mother was buried next to his grave. It was another warm summer day and many of the same friends gathered afterward at Aunt Marie's house for the traditional salad and coffee and dessert, just as we had done for Jim. Celebrating life, acknowledging death and imagining the reunion of mother and son.

Grief and Children

Helping my children through this land of mourning has been difficult and bewildering. My own grief was enormous; needing to help them with theirs as well was overwhelming at times. If only we could have done it consecutively: first to resolve my own grief, finding my own way through this valley; then to lead them. Never having been this way before, I felt I was like a lost shepherd. But the help of caring friends and competent professionals has been invaluable, and we have all come a very long way.

As the books I read had indicated, regressive behavior in young children is to be expected. Lapses into baby talk, even soiling or bed-wetting are common. Little ones have a harder time identifying their grief, and it can take many different forms. Is it simply an expression of that deep desire to return to those early days when Daddy was still with us? I have tried to help Ethan find words for those longings, for his pain and sadness, encouraging him to identify it and talk about it. We looked for ways to ease that hurt, to bring comfort. Hugging and touching and quiet words can help take the jagged edge from pain. We found that for all of us soft foods—yogurt, soup, puddings—somehow seemed to have a soothing effect.

Adolescence brings its own innate chaos and it has been difficult (although necessary to try) to distinguish between the grieving and the inevitable struggles of growing up. Soon after Jim's death, Jessie's body began to make those drastic changes from girl to young woman, heedless of her own preferences.

Puberty is bewildering at the best of times, but to have lost her daddy—affirmer, admirer, encourager—at this crucial point has made these years particularly difficult ones for Jess. Words and hugs have been major ingredients in her growing toward wholeness. I have tried to find other men who would do what Jim might have done had he been here: a friend took her out for a very elegant dinner to celebrate her sixth-grade graduation.

Jeff's pain has been less evident to me, but it appears he has come to terms with his father's death. "When Daddy died, I decided it was time for me to grow up. So I did," he told me many months later. His interactions with Ethan, particularly, showed a distinctly paternal bent. I asked him not to believe it if he heard the well-intended suggestion, "You're the man of the family now." That may be more true as time passes, but I felt it was an unreasonable burden for a twelve-year-old.

Even though at times they wear their grief so visibly, I am coming to realize that some of it has been submerged, perhaps in an effort to protect me. I don't want that and have told them as much. "I'm supposed to take care of you. Please don't be afraid of sharing your hurt with me." But at the same time I must acknowledge to myself and to them that this is a brokenness which I can't fix for any of us. Recent conversations with a number of adult friends have convinced me that trying to protect one's parent can be a common theme of adolescence.

Hugs. Struggling for words. And listening. More hugs. I have tried to model for them some of the work of grieving, allowing them to see my sadness and tears without being overwhelmed by them. I am certain that I have not always done that well.

Regular times alone with each child (breakfast or supper out, or trips to Amy's Ice Cream Shop) have been valuable in maintaining communication. These are usually times of conversation about ordinary, everyday life with only occasional significant conversations. (The really important stuff seems to get discussed in side-by-side conversations, while peeling carrots, or stirring the soup, or making beds together, or riding in the car.)

Maintaining old family traditions and building new ones seem to be important components of the "glue" of family building—and rebuilding. Familiar places and people and events can be reassuring when so much of life has suddenly become frighteningly unfamiliar.

I see growth and healing. But it isn't finished. And I want desperately for them and for me to emerge from this crisis time with enough health and wholeness to be able to move eagerly through life, living and loving well.

Facing the Future

While I have found single parenting to be much harder, it is at the same time much simpler: only one person sets the direction, makes the decisions. No compromises with another authority figure. But it is lonely. Exhausting sometimes. And I have a strong tendency to lose my perspective under stress.

Though I would like to have that partnership again, quite frankly, I have a hard time imagining what it would be like to "blend" a man (or perhaps even a family) into our family. I'd like to marry again, but even if I don't, if I never have that again, I know that in those years of loving and being loved by Jim, I have had more than many people hope for in a lifetime.

I am surprisingly content with my single state—most of the time. After four years, life without Jim is manageable, familiar. But sometimes when I've been drawn into the warm circle of a friend's good marriage, allowing me to see up close the delight of intimacy, the deep joy of loving another, the companionship, the communication, I am reminded of what I've been missing. And I remember the struggle and conflict and compromise which can scour and buff and polish; the sharing of life's everyday occurrences, both momentous and insignificant. I long for that again, with a deep, aching loneliness rarely acknowledged even to myself.

Choice-Making, Risk-Taking

But I am seeing that life is full of choices if I look for them. At some times and seasons of our lives that is more true than at others. And some choices are mutually exclusive: Marrying one man eliminates all the other possibilities; choosing to have children greatly reduces the likelihood of having a high-powered career, at least for a while.

I think one of the dangers of our relatively affluent and materialistic Western society is that we stop considering our options. We can become so caught up in the familiar routines, in doing and having more, that we get locked into self-perpetuating patterns which dramatically limit our alternatives. We just do "the next thing"—faster, and more often.

As a family we have discussed all this any number of times, and we've agreed to work at encouraging one another to consider our alternatives, investigate our options, make some unusual choices when we can. We've determined not to live in a way that simply follows the path of least resistance.

Now I know that life can be shorter than I expected, and I don't intend to let it slip by me. As Garrison Keillor's mother always says, "Life is what you make it. You'd better make the most of it." That tenuous balance in living well: security and risk. Wanting the safety and comfort of the familiar but knowing that growing and loving and really living always entail a measure of risk.

Unique is not necessarily better—we must carefully make the best choices we can. But I want always to be aware of the fact that I do have choices.

Faith and Grief

But sometimes even our best choices have unexpected endings, a fact with which I have become painfully familiar. And then it matters what kind of God we know. When it felt like my world was going to pieces (as the psalmist described it in Psalm 46, "the earth fell away and the mountains tumbled into the sea"), I knew I was loved by the God who is in control. The One who created the universe loves us and intends good for us.

In the early years of my marriage I had, providentially, read many books about loss and grief, always reminding God that I was willing to help others through their crisis times. But in my prayers I also shared the desire to be spared this anguish in my own life.

For whatever reason, God chose not to spare us this deep pain. And in those agonizing early days, I knew enough about God's character to be able to say, "Someday I will be able to look back and say even out of this God has brought good." I can't imagine what good or how that could possibly be true; it goes contrary to everything I feel right now. But I choose to believe the truth of what I've been taught all these years about God's character. Someday it will be true.

Four years later, I can see good that God has done in our lives. Had I been given the choice, I would never have chosen this. But I am grateful for the growth that I see in all of us, although I would have wished it to come in another way. What we have learned in these four years about ourselves, about our world, about God is of great value. I feel confident that Jim would like the persons we are becoming.

The Scriptures teach that God will use suffering to build character and to purify our faith (see Rom 5 and 1 Pet 1). I can't presume to know all that he is doing in our lives; that he has allowed us to see a small part of it, I'm grateful.

Those strong words in Isaiah ring true for me. That he will "bind up the brokenhearted . . . comfort all who mourn, and provide for those who grieve. To bestow on them a crown of beauty instead of ashes, the oil of gladness instead of mourning, and a garment of praise instead of a spirit of despair. They will be called oaks of righteousness, a planting of the Lord for the display of his splendor."

Change. Growth. Healing. Beauty for ashes. Gladness for

mourning. Praise out of despair. But the last phrase is all-important: that it might be to his glory, "for the display of his splendor."

August 1988